Miss Wh

DNA
GCSE Student
Guide

Methuen Drama publications for GCSE students

Available and forthcoming

GCSE Student Editions

Willy Russell's *Blood Brothers*
Simon Stephens's *The Curious Incident of the Dog in the Night-Time*
Charlotte Keatley's *My Mother Said I Never Should*
Shelagh Delaney's *A Taste of Honey*

GCSE Student Guides

Willy Russell's *Blood Brothers* by Ros Merkin
Simon Stephens's *The Curious Incident of the Dog in the Night-Time* by Jacqueline Bolton
Dennis Kelly's *DNA* by Maggie Inchley
Alan Bennett's *The History Boys* by Steve Nicholson
J. B. Priestley's *An Inspector Calls* by Philip Roberts
R. C. Sherriff's *Journey's End* by Andrew Maunder
Charlotte Keatley's *My Mother Said I Never Should* by Sophie Bush
Shelagh Delaney's *A Taste of Honey* by Kate Whittaker

DNA

GCSE Student Guide

MAGGIE INCHLEY

Series Editor: Jenny Stevens

Bloomsbury Methuen Drama
An imprint of Bloomsbury Publishing Plc

BLOOMSBURY
LONDON · OXFORD · NEW YORK · NEW DELHI · SYDNEY

Bloomsbury Methuen Drama

An imprint of Bloomsbury Publishing Plc

Imprint previously known as Methuen Drama

50 Bedford Square	1385 Broadway
London	New York
WC1B 3DP	NY 10018
UK	USA

www.bloomsbury.com

BLOOMSBURY, METHUEN DRAMA and the Diana logo are trademarks of Bloomsbury Publishing Plc

British Library Cataloguing-in-Publication Data
A catalogue record for this book is available from the British Library.

ISBN:	PB:	978-1-4742-3254-8
	ePDF:	978-1-4742-3255-5
	epub:	978-1-4742-3257-9

Library of Congress Cataloging-in-Publication Data
A catalog record for this book is available from the Library of Congress

Series: GCSE Student Guides

Typeset by RefineCatch Limited, Bungay, Suffolk
Printed and bound in Great Britain

For all my partners in crime. You know who you are.

CONTENTS

ACKNOWLEDGEMENTS

In researching and writing this book, I have been grateful for the help, knowledge and insight of Anthony Banks. In addition to giving a heartfelt acknowledgement of his contribution, I would also like to thank Dennis Kelly, James Alexandrou and Ruby Bentall for so generously giving interviews. Throughout the process I have been fortunate to have had the encouragement, wisdom and support of editors, Jenny Stevens and Anna Brewer. Thanks, too, for the permissions granted by Libby Purves, Tanika Gupta and Laurie Hanna.

This book is a partly a product of many years of teaching in schools and universities, and I am indebted to each of my past colleagues, students and pupils for the privilege of working with them. To any of you who may pick up this book, know that you have helped me to write it.

CHAPTER ONE

The Play

Introduction

Dennis Kelly wrote *DNA* for young people of your age to perform, and for people of all ages to see in the theatre.

While you are reading, think about *DNA* not only as a text, but also as a play that is performed. Try to imagine it. What would this play look like in a theatre? Who are the *characters*, and what situations are they in? How would they think, feel and move? What would they be wearing, and what would their *costumes* say about them? It is also good to imagine the design of the play. That is, how it would look in the theatre. How would the *set* take you to the locations of the play, and what kind of mood or atmosphere would it create? How would *lighting* and *sound effects* contribute to the atmosphere of each scene, and help to tell its story? As you study the play, take any opportunities you can to perform scenes, as this will help you to understand how it works as drama.

In this guide, I will frequently mention Kelly, the playwright. For your English Literature GCSE it will be important to show an understanding of the many choices Kelly has made about the play, and the ways he has planned and constructed it. As part of your studying, get into the habit of talking and writing about Kelly and how he presents the characters, the plot and the themes in *DNA*.

Plays are often divided into sections called acts. As you are reading the play, you will notice that Kelly does not use this traditional term. In the text, the reader sees only One, Two, Three and Four. For ease of reference in this guide, I have used the word *section* rather than act to refer to the four parts of *DNA*, and the fourteen *scenes* that they contain. Within the sections, Kelly has shown a change of scene just with three asterisks. This suggests how in performance the action of each scene blends quickly into the next, even though it takes place in a different location. A challenge for the designer and director of any production of *DNA* is to make these changes of locations happen quickly, without holding up the action of the play.

As you are studying *DNA*, you will need to think in detail not only about its performance and audience, but also about the *language* of the play. What does each character say and how do they speak? How is language used to create tension or suspense? Pay close attention to the *stage directions*. These are a very important part of the script. Through the stage directions, Kelly gives very important instructions that will tell us about location, action, dialogue and plot.

If I use a word in this guide that you do not understand, you can look it up in the glossary. Do not be afraid to ask your teacher if you are still unsure, or if the word is not included. Try to get used to any new words by using them yourself when you talk or write about the play. By doing this, you will expand your vocabulary and be able to write about *DNA* in a way that will meet the requirements of your GCSE examination.

I hope you enjoy studying *DNA* for your GCSE as much as I have enjoyed writing this guide. It's a great play. Good luck!

Overview

This overview section gives you a brief summary of each scene. It is there to help to give you a quick check on which characters are in each scene, what happens in it, and some of its themes. It is not there to replace your own reading: you will need to get to know each scene in detail, and to develop your own thoughts and interpretations about each one.

Section one

Kelly opens the play in a street, giving no other details as to specific town or city or time of day. The tense dialogue between Jan and Mark projects the reader or audience member immediately into a dramatic and deadly serious situation. A death is revealed as the inciting but as yet mysterious incident.

Changing the setting to a field, Kelly introduces us to Phil and to Leah. Phil spends the entire scene entirely silent, eating an ice cream, while Leah tries to get a response from him, and speaks of the 'brutal terror' that everyone is living in (12). When Jan and Mark arrive at the end of the scene, Mark announces, 'We need to talk to you'. Leah's response, 'Oh, shit', heightens the sense that something very serious is happening (12).

The third scene is much longer and more complex, moving the action to a wood, and involving the whole ensemble cast. Only Adam is absent, and the entire scene is structured around the group's reactions to what has happened to him. At first, John Tate tries to allay Lou and Danny's fears, to exert his authority, and impress upon the other teenagers the need for silence. After Richard arrives with the '*grinning*' Cathy and tearful Brian, John Tate forces the friends to acknowledge his leadership (15). The audience at last hears what happened to Adam when the arrival of Jan, Mark, Phil and Leah leads to a chilling description from Mark of Adam's apparently fatal fall. When Phil speaks for the first time in the play, it is to issue instructions for an elaborate plan to fake DNA evidence that will divert attention from their own involvement in what the teenagers (and audience) believe is Adam's death.

The final scene of the first section returns to the field for the second of Leah and Phil's duologues. While Leah muses on the differences in behaviour between bonobos and chimps, Phil says nothing. His only action is to open and eat a packet of crisps. In what seems like an effort to test his capacity for empathy, Leah attempts to strangle herself. With her final words, 'Trouble now', Kelly creates a cliffhanger ending, ominously suggesting that something worse is yet to come (28).

Section two

Using a pattern of structural repetition, Kelly begins the second section just as he did the first, using the same location and characters. As in the play's opening scene, there is a short, tense exchange between Jan and Mark. The scene introduces a complication into the action as Mark reveals, 'He's not going' (29). The audience is left wondering to whom and to what Mark's comment refers.

The second scene of the second section continues the pattern of structural repetitions. As in Leah and Phil's first field scene, Leah speaks to a silent, junk-food eating Phil. The scene further establishes Leah's character as a natural and moral philosopher, and reveals that the group has been carrying out Phil's instructions. There is a growing strangeness and darkness to the play's tone, as the themes of killing and fakeness are developed. Again, Jan and Mark appear at the end of the scene. When Jan announces, 'We need to talk', the audience is sucked in further to the story, and suspense grows over what has gone wrong (32).

In this second of Kelly's series of three ensemble wood scenes, Lou and Danny bring Leah and a muffin-eating Phil the news that the man who has supposedly killed Adam has been found. The group is faced with a rapidly snowballing sequence of events about which they must decide to speak or keep silent. Richard and Cathy enter, revealing that they have faked DNA evidence to link a postman to Adam's disappearance. When Jan and Mark then arrive with Brian, who is refusing to identify the postman falsely, the group appear to be 'screwed', as Lou repeatedly insists. In a reprise of the action in the first wood scene, Phil's first words are to suggest a solution. When he threatens Brian that he will join Adam at the bottom of the shaft, the boy agrees to go to the police. All the teenagers choose or are forced to become complicit in the cover up.

Completing the second cycle of the pattern established in the first section, Section Two ends with another field scene with Leah and Phil. Leah has an epiphany, realizing that they seem to be caught in a repeated pattern of behaviour. Phil's only word in the scene, 'No', is to deny her belief that, 'If you can change one thing you can change the world' (43).

Section three

In common with all the sections, Jan and Mark start Section Three in a street. This time, Mark reveals to a shocked and bemused Jan that 'Cathy found him in the woods' (45). Typically enticing, Kelly teases the audience with this further complication in the plot.

Arriving in the field with a suitcase, Leah tells Phil she is 'running away' (46). She reveals that Brian is on medication, that John Tate has not been seen, and that the postman is spending his life in prison. When Jan and Mark arrive and announce, 'You really, really better come with us', they disturb Phil's eating of his carefully made jam waffle (48). Leah goes with them to the wood.

The third of the three ensemble wood scenes is the darkest part of *DNA*. Kelly uses the scene to show how far some members of the group will go to protect themselves, and the extent to which Phil is able to threaten or manipulate the others to carry out his orders. When Phil greets the strange tramp-like boy as Adam, the audience realizes that the group have been mistaken in believing him dead. Here we see the teenagers at their most helpless, and deeply incriminated by their actions and complicity in the plot to frame the postman. Phil responds to their repeated cries of, 'What are we gonna do?', by showing a 'game' to Brian and Cathy where a plastic bag is placed over Brian's head. Horrified, the audience realizes that Phil is teaching them how to suffocate Adam. Phil is deaf to Leah's pleas as Cathy and Brian exit with Adam. Neither Richard nor Danny appear in this scene.

Back in the field in the immediate and deathly silent aftermath, Phil tries to comfort the quietly crying Leah with a Starburst, and by putting his arm around her. In a reversal of earlier scenes, Leah says nothing, eventually spitting out her sweet and storming off. Phil is left alone, calling after her.

Section four

The final section starts with the now familiar street scene between Jan and Mark. The plot is progressed by Mark's revelation, 'she's gone', and as the play begins to reach its end it is not hard for the audience to guess that they are referring to Leah. Jan's final question, 'Does Phil know?' sets up what will be the final scene of the play (62–3).

In this concluding field scene, Phil remains silent. For the first time, he is not eating, a sign that he has become withdrawn and unhappy. Richard, who now accompanies Phil rather than Leah, brings news of the other teenagers' lives, and tries to cajole Phil into coming back to the group. The final scene cuts short the pattern of locations that Kelly has established. This disruption is unsettling, contributing to an uncertain and ambivalent feeling at the end.

Things to do

1 Work in a pair to make a time-line for *DNA*. Mark on your time-line the main events of the play, and also events that you think happened before the play started. Ask your teacher if you can use the classroom walls or corridors to

make a display. As a class, discuss what might happen if you extended the time-line. What might happen after the end of *DNA*?

2 Imagine that a new edition of *DNA* is going to be published. Use a computer to design the book jacket and write the blurb for the back cover. Try to make sure your design captures something important about the play, and that your blurb is an enticing as possible.

Contexts

GCSE English Literature requires you to show your knowledge and understanding of wider contexts (AO3). This section will help you to find ways to include information and ideas to show some of these. Also see the 'Related work' section for ideas for AO3.

Connections

Connections is an annual festival of new plays commissioned by the National Theatre (NT) for youth theatres and schools. It has been running since 1995. Every year, Connections commissions ten adult writers to write ten new plays for young people, aged 13–19 years old. Schools and youth theatre groups work with their teacher or director to put on one of the plays in their school, church hall or other home venue. This production then becomes part of the Connections Festival and is performed at a professional theatre in the local area. The final stage of the festival takes place at the NT itself, where a performance group for each play is invited to participate. The project aims to provide 'succinct and potent' plays for young people, and to provide scripts that will suit the demands of busy youth theatres (AQA, 2009). Short plays with running times of under an hour are deliberately commissioned. Over the years, the project has produced more than 140 plays by adult writers such as Mark Ravenhill, David Mamet and Dennis Kelly. In 2015, there were 27 partner theatres and over 25,000 audience members saw the plays (About Us). *DNA* was commissioned in 2005, and was subsequently given a full professional production by the NT in 2008.

Production history

2005   Kelly commissioned for NT Connections.

2006   *DNA* drafted and workshopped.

2007   First production of *DNA* by youth theatre at NT as part of the Connections Festival.

2008   *DNA* staged professionally at the NT, along with Roy Williams' *Baby Girl* and Lin Coghlan's *The Miracle*. Directed by Paul Miller.

2012   National tour of over 20 English theatres, including Manchester Royal Exchange, Sheffield Crucible, the egg, Bath and Hull Truck Theatre. Directed by Anthony Banks.

2012   *DNA* becomes a GCSE English Literature set text

Drama about young people

The 2000s saw a big increase in the amount of dramas on film and in the theatre that represented the lives of young people. Previously, the BBC series *Grange Hill*, which ran from 1978 to 2008, was ground breaking in its realistic portrayal of school life. *Hollyoaks* started on Channel 4 in 1995, with a large cast of young people. *Skins*, created by Jamie Brittain, which focuses on sixth form characters, began on E4 in 2007 (the same year that *DNA* was first performed). In these new programmes, young characters had major roles, rather than only appearing momentarily.

In the 2000s, an increasing number of mainstream theatres commissioned adult writers to write plays for young people. In 2004, the NT produced *The History Boys,* putting on stage a group of grammar school boys played by young actors. At the Traverse in Edinburgh, David Greig's *Yellow Moon* (2007) told the story of Scottish teenage runaways, and Tanika Gupta's *White Boy* (2007) at the Soho Theatre in London portrayed the lives of black, white and mixed race teenagers. At the NT, the Connections programme was part of this increase in drama focusing on the lives of young people. The 2005 season included Mark Ravenhill's *Citizenship*, which portrayed a teenage boy coming to terms with his sexuality, and Enda Walsh's *Chatroom*, which explored on-line bullying. In many of these plays there are very few or no adult characters at all, and young people frequently seem to be isolated, abandoned, or left to work things out for themselves. Many of the plays do not represent young people as particularly happy. In fact, the 2006 series of New Connections plays at the NT caused one theatre critic to comment on their portrayal of 'teenage angst and insecurity', and another on the 'suffering, cruelty and depression' of teenage life (Billington 2006 and Marmion 2006). *DNA* is no exception in these respects. One of its major characters, Leah, is preoccupied by the way her schoolmates seem to pretend to be happy, rather than actually being so. In spite of this, much of this drama is also humorous, lively and uplifting, and it was very much enjoyed by huge numbers of teenagers who flocked to theatres to see the plays that represented the lives of people of their own age.

Things to do

Make a list of TV programmes you know or plays you have seen where young people are the main characters. Do you think that they give a negative, positive or balanced view of young people?

The 2000s

DNA was first performed in 2007, but in the text Kelly does not specify the year in which the action of the play is imagined to take place. There are no explicit references to actual historical events. In fact, the timelessness of the play is deliberate. Kelly's main concerns are the way that young people can behave in groups and in human nature, not in showing us what life was like in the mid-2000s. Plays and other types of writing however cannot escape from history all together. In spite of Kelly's avoidance of mentioning specific historical events, his play contains suggestions of the matters that were preoccupying and affecting people in the 2000s.

Adults have often been very concerned about the behaviour of young people, especially when they are not under adult supervision. In the British newspapers, young people have been called 'hoodies', 'chavs', or 'feral', and fears are frequently expressed regarding binge-drinking, violence and delinquency. In the 2000s the government and police used measures to control the behaviour of young people. These included Anti-Social Behaviour Orders (ASBOs), first used in 1999. ASBOs can restrict the movements of anyone from the age of ten upwards who is deemed to behave in an antisocial way. Dispersal Orders were introduced in 2003. These give the police the right to disperse a group of two or more if they are considered to be harassing, intimidating, alarming or distressing a member of the public. In 2011, shortly before *DNA* was revived for a national tour, there was a wave of rioting across England. Much of the unrest was blamed on young people, and in the aftermath the involvement of the young was intensely scrutinized. Asked by a journalist about the links of the behaviour of the young people in the riots with *DNA*, Kelly remarked that the characters 'have an understanding that what they're doing is wrong, but they carry on regardless' (Kelly in Bowie-Sell 2012).

In the twentieth century, several types of technology developed that could be used to deter and monitor criminal behaviour. These included Closed Circuit Television (CCTV), a system first used in Germany in 1942 to monitor the launch of V-2 rockets. It became common in UK cities in the 1990s and 2000s, and began to be used in schools as a means to combat bullying and monitor behaviour. In Tanika Gupta's play, *White Boy,* which like *DNA* was first produced in 2007, the action of the play takes place under CCTV monitors near the school gates. In *DNA,* the gang has found a hide out in the woods, away from this constant surveillance and adult monitoring, where they seem free to act as they choose.

By the 2000s, in combatting and investigating crime, the police were relying heavily on Deoxyribonucleic Acid (DNA) Profiling in Forensics. This is the use of science to gather evidence that can be used in a court of law. DNA evidence is frequently seen in TV crime dramas, such as the North American series *CSI: Crime Scene Investigation,* playing an important part in catching and convicting criminals. DNA is a molecule that stores biological information unique to each individual person. The development of genetic profiling meant that forensic scientists could use DNA in blood, semen, skin, saliva or hair found at a crime scene to identify a suspect. In the 1990s and 2000s DNA databases were developed, which helped investigators check traces found at crime scenes against their records. In 2001 it became legal to keep DNA on record, even if a person was found to be innocent. This law raises issues of civil liberties and privacy, as many people feel that the police should not be keeping the DNA of innocent adults and young people. In *DNA,* the teenagers' plan to plant DNA evidence is surprisingly successful, and leads to the conviction of an innocent man.

Things to do

Find out more about DNA. Produce a list of 10 interesting facts (not necessarily the first ones you find).

Discuss

1 What are the benefits of DNA databases for society?
2 Are there any risks or dangers to relying on DNA to fight crime?

Related to the issue of surveillance are the rights of the individual. Although we seem to live as free individuals, there are laws, measures and technologies that regulate and control behaviour. At times, tensions between individual rights and state powers cause discontent, and adjustments are necessary in laws and culture. In the 2000s, new laws aimed to protect national security were introduced following the attack on the Twin Towers in the USA. The UK government introduced the Anti-Terrorism, Crime and Security Act, 2001, which gave the police the right to indefinite detention of non-British nationals without trial. The Terrorism Act of 2006, following the bombings in London in 2005, allowed for people suspected of terrorist offences to be detained without charge for up to 28 days. *DNA* is not explicitly about terrorism, but it is deeply concerned with the 'disappearance' of an innocent individual and the safety of the whole group. The dilemma is very clearly stated by Phil, 'What's more important; one person or everyone' (58).

Finally, the 2000s saw great public anxiety around a number of other global issues. The planet was affected by huge disasters such as the Indian Ocean tsunami in 2004 that killed over 250 million people, and in 2005 by Hurricane Katrina, which flooded New Orleans. Many scientists and ordinary people became extremely concerned about climate change, and the long-term effects of the pursuit of economic growth on global warming. In *DNA,* Leah's concerns over 'nuclear waste and global warming' seem to raise a global anxiety that she links to a lack of happiness in the world (30). Leah tries to get it into perspective by thinking about the place of humanity in the universe, 'It's life that upsets the natural order. It's us that's the anomaly' (31).

Teenage gangs and behaviour

In 2004, a US university study claimed, 'Gangs are a major social problem', and found a strong correlation between gang membership and delinquent behaviour (Gordon, 55). The study claimed that peer pressure plays a strong role in the way gang members behave. In the UK, there was concern that gang culture was spreading amongst young people. Incidents, such as the Damilola Taylor case in 2000, where a ten-year-old boy was killed by a group of young people, as well as the deaths in a drive-by shooting of teenage girls Letisha Shakespeare and Charlene Ellis in 2003, fuelled public concern. Here are some extracts from a 2007 article from *The Mirror*, where the journalist reports on a real teenage gang in South London.

Daily Mirror, 'Teen Gangs of Britain', by Laurie Hanna

Teenage gangsters caught in Britain's rising tide of street violence are locked into their lifestyle by a tribal code of honour that insists: 'You're one of us until you die.'

One 14-year-old told a *Mirror* investigation into street gang culture that many members are threatened with death if they even consider quitting.

He said: 'Once you're in, there's no way out – 'cos if you leave, people will be asking you questions, see?'

The *Mirror* spent five days on the streets of Dulwich, South London, with one of them – the Uptown Boys – to discover why so many teenagers are ensnared by this sinister and dangerous world.

As dusk falls the gang members begin to assemble – all wearing their distinctive uniform of expensive trainers, low-slung jeans, hoodies and caps.

F-Man is 20 but he's been in jail twice, for GBH and kidnap. He says: 'Being part of a gang is like having an extended family.

'We all trust each other. There's about 15 of us in the inner circle, the hardcore. If I wanted, I could get my hands on whatever weapons I wanted. Guns, knives, whatever.'

F-Man says many young kids join gangs out of boredom. He adds: 'The problem is, yeah, there's nothing to do around here so they find things to do.'

For others, the gang is an alternative family – one that provides protection and a feeling of belonging that they do not get at home. The 14-year-old says: 'It's better to be on the inside than on the outside.

'You know not to mess with certain people because they're in a gang. Being in a gang puts fear in people. Say you've seen someone on the bus before and they're looking at you in way like "Yeah, you gonna do something to me?"'

HANNA 2007

Things to do

Use the article above to think about why teenagers join gangs. Highlight any references that suggest the members stay in the group from *loyalty* or *fear*. Find references to *status*, *trust* and *family*. Finally, how does the article suggest adults could help prevent teenagers forming gangs? Use your findings to reach a conclusion: what are the reasons young people might join and stay in a gang?

Themes

Gang power dynamics

One of the major themes of *DNA* is the behaviour of teenagers in groups. Dennis Kelly uses this to explore human nature in extreme circumstances. Kelly is not describing a real gang, like the one in the article in the 'Contexts' section above, but one that he has made from his imagination for performance in a fictional play. Nevertheless, it is useful to have some background knowledge on how groups often function in the real world.

In 2005, the Jill Dando Institute (JDI) identified three types of gang. The first is a 'peer group', which is a small, unorganized group whose members share the same space and a common history. Any involvement in low-level crime will not be important to the identity of the group. The second type is a 'gang'. Gangs are mostly comprised of street based groups of young people for whom crime and violence is an essential part of the group's identity. Thirdly, an 'organized criminal group' is a group of individuals who are involved in crime for personal gain, and who operate in the illegal marketplace (Gang Culture).

The JDI research also found that gangs are often 'hierarchical communities', and identified the various roles that individuals play within groups or gangs. These roles consist of 'gang leaders', who determine strategies and plan activities but do not get involved in committing offences; 'gang workers', who are established gang members caught up in the running of the business; and 'foot soldiers', who are often the youngest members of the gang and most at risk of becoming involved in violent crime.

It would be a big mistake to try to fit the teenage gang in *DNA* neatly into any of these categories, but the JDI descriptions are useful in helping us to ask questions about the kind of gang that Kelly presents, and the way it evolves and changes. Does the gang in *DNA* give the teenagers a sense of identity? How do its power dynamics work? What is the role of peer pressure? To what extent are the gang's violent or criminal actions organized and planned?

A personal response to characters or themes in drama should be based on evidence of the circumstances presented in the play. Let's start with thinking about how Kelly presents the teenagers' lives. Some details suggest that the teenagers come from every day families. Through Leah, we learn that Mark's mum is having a baby, that there is an Asda in the vicinity, and what she has seen on television. The young people do not seem to be neglected or marginalized, but Kelly's choice to present the world of the gang allows the teenagers to be seen without adults. Leah's reference to 'cheap ice cream' at Adam's parties suggests a class consciousness and the possible root of the bullying that the gang inflicts (58).

One of John Tate's ways of maintaining his leadership is to give to the gang members a sense of identity and belonging. The character points out to everyone that life in the group is 'better' than before, that everyone wants 'to be us', and to 'come here to the woods' (17). John Tate reminds Lou of the high status the group of teenagers enjoy at their school, where everyone 'respects' and is 'scared' of her (13–14). His description is reminiscent of the 'fear' with which the South London gang member claims to be regarded by members of the public in the article above.

Life in the group is far from comfortable, and there are many moments when it is fragile, full of tensions and rivalries. Being in the group may give its members kudos, but it is deeply undermining of the teenagers' emotional and psychological health. Leah starts the play describing the 'brutal terror' and the 'fear that everyone here lives in' (12). From her descriptions, it is possible to tell that healthy and respectful relationships are not the norm. 'Remember last month, Dan threatened to kill Cathy?' (32). The group itself seems to offer little genuine, close and caring friendship. In the first field scene, Leah reveals not only that 'I haven't got friends', but that Phil doesn't either (11).

In *DNA*, Kelly explores how the power in the gang operates through a hierarchy, with each member having more or less status depending on their role in the group. Leah's opening address to John for example, 'Can I just say John, that we haven't done anything', reveals Leah's sense of her own low status, and John Tate's role as an authority figure to whom she feels she has to tell the truth (19). The dynamics of the group allow stronger members to exert peer pressure on others, encouraging more vulnerable teenagers to conform to irresponsible or dangerous behaviour. The clearest example of the damaging effects of peer pressure are with Adam, who steals vodka, lets the group punch and burn him, and runs across the motorway in a desperate effort to be accepted.

The power dynamics in *DNA* are not static, and the changes in leadership that take place suggest the gang outlives its individuals. When at a loss to know what to do about Adam's fall, John Tate approaches Phil, 'Cathy says you're clever. What do we do?' (23). The moment marks the point at which John Tate effectively stands down, relinquishing the leadership of the group to Phil. By the end of the play, Richard reports that Cathy has taken over, and her regime sounds more brutal than ever. Kelly suggests endlessly evolving patterns to gang life, and that the gang is somehow more resilient than its individual members.

Human nature

Another of the major themes of the play is human nature and behaviour in extreme circumstances. This is an aspect of the play that recalls William Golding's portrayal of a group of schoolboys stranded on an island in his 1954 novel *Lord of the Flies* (about which you can read more in the 'Related works' and 'Critical reception' sections). The theme raises age-old questions concerning whether humans function according to fixed aspects of their biology, or how far behaviour is a result of social factors. Significantly, this relates to the title of the play, *DNA*. Are humans a mass of biological impulses, or do we have choices regarding the way they behave? Is it in the DNA of humanity to be cruel, and to act selfishly? Or are we naturally inclined to be empathetic, and to work together to build a civilized society?

The theme of human nature is raised most clearly by Leah's musings on the nature of chimps and bonobos. These invite comparison with the teenagers themselves, and the hierarchical way that their gang is organized. The speech is positioned in the play immediately after the scene in which the audience hears of the horrific bullying of Adam and his 'death' by stoning at the hands of the gang. 'Chimps are evil', Leah says, 'They kill and sometimes torture each other to find a better position within the social structure' (26). Her next comment almost seems to describe the incident in the wood, 'A chimp'll just find itself outside of a group and before he knows what's happening it's being hounded to death by the others.' According to the documentary Leah has seen, however, it is bonobos rather than chimps who are humans' closest living relatives. This is due to 'the tiniest change in their DNA'. Unlike chimps, these monkeys are friendly, and can feel the pain of others. 'Such sadness in their intelligent eyes. Empathy.' With typical lack of sentimentality however, Kelly avoids idealizing bonobos: they're 'Sex mad', Leah tells us, and concludes the monkeys are 'disgusting' (27). Her comment could suggest, that as bonobos' living relatives, humans are too.

In *DNA*, it is undeniable that the audience hears about some of the most reprehensible aspects of human behaviour. Kelly comes closest to portraying the teenagers as a feral pack in Mark's account of the bullying of Adam. Afterwards, the teenagers frame an innocent man and murder a boy with a plastic bag to save their own skins. Even so, Kelly suggests that the behaviour of the teenagers is unplanned and thoughtless, rather than malicious. Mark's account of the events suggests that even the stone throwing happened 'just for the laugh' (23). What is more, we do not actually see these events happening. Rather like the off-stage violence in a Greek tragedy, the baiting and stoning of Adam is reported by Jan and Mark, and is not portrayed directly. Instead, the audience is witness to a frightened group of teenagers, relating a dreadful event that has got out of hand, and about which they believe they will be in deep trouble. Anthony Banks, who commissioned and directed the play, has emphasized the spontaneity of the teenagers' actions. James Alexandrou, the actor who played Phil in the 2012 production of DNA, also saw Phil's solution as a spontaneous response to the dire circumstances that the teenagers find themselves in (see 'Behind the Scenes' interviews).

According to reviewer Louise Lewis, Kelly's teenagers are 'anything but innocent', but their characters retain a 'youthful naivety' (Lewis 2012). The comment describes the apparently contradictory responses it is possible to feel about Kelly's group of characters. Much of the time, the teenagers seem needy or vulnerable, and desperately in need of leadership and guidance. The repetition of 'What are we going to do?' by almost all the characters makes them seem naive and unresourceful, rather than calculatingly evil. In this light, it becomes impossible to see the group's actions as planned or malicious. Lou's line, 'We're screwed', indicates the trouble the teenagers think they are in, and the sense of impotence that they feel. Although there are moments of tension and challenge, they are largely passive and obedient with Phil, and capable of working together, however misguidedly. Throughout the play, it is only Leah's decision to leave the group that seems to suggest the possibility for an active ethical choice to break away from this pattern of group behaviour.

DNA resists giving the audience an easy answer to the question of human nature. Instead, Kelly gives us more ambiguous portraits of his teenage characters. 'I think that there are such things in the world as truly good people and truly bad people but they are tiny percentages at the end of a great big spectrum . . . the rest of us are just somewhere in the big grey area in the middle' (Kelly, in Bowie-Sell 2012).

Discuss

1 Do you think Kelly's teenagers are more like bonobos or chimps? Find examples from the play to support your view.

2 Where do you think cruel and violent behaviour comes from? Is it innate in human nature? Or does it arise from the ways that we make our society?

3 In this book, I have sometimes referred to the teenagers as a 'gang'. At other times I have used the word 'group'. What do these two different words suggest about their nature and behaviour? Do you think I should have made a definite choice for one or the other?

Things to do

In the final scene of the play, Richard says he has been caught up in a 'big wind of fluff' and felt like he was an alien sitting in a cloud. Imagine you are an alien and have been hovering over the street, field and wood. Make a list of the main incidents you have seen, then send a report back to your home planet about the young human people on Planet Earth.

Covering up

DNA is full of stories, and some of the most dramatic moments of the play come from them. Some of the stories are based on things that happened off-stage, such as Mark's account of the bullying of Adam, or Adam's faltering but spellbinding account of this own 're-birth'. The most central story in the play, the story that the teenagers tell about Adam's disappearance, is a fabrication, designed to cover up their own involvement.

DNA revolves around decisions that the teenagers make about telling stories and keeping silent. Through these decisions, Kelly explores the practical, ethical and psychological consequences of decisions to speak or to say nothing. Often the stories in *DNA* dramatically change the way the audience feels, or draw them in further to the play's narrative – itself, of course, a story constructed by Kelly.

In the first wood scene, as the teenagers struggle to come to terms with Adam's death, John Tate insists on silence, banning the word 'dead'. He challenges Lou and Danny to, 'Say it and see what happens' (15). Lou and Danny 'say nothing', but when Richard turns up and announces, 'He's dead', Kelly suggests the difficulties in keeping things quiet (15).

Phil also emphasizes silence. As a rule the character says almost nothing. In the field scenes he seems mysterious or enigmatic, sitting in an open field contemplating existence. When he does set his coke can down to open his mouth, it is to come up with the false story of Adam's death based on the apparent truth of DNA evidence. The story that the teenagers will fabricate together is planned brilliantly, but requires them to keep silent: 'Keep your mouths shut. Tell no-one or we'll all go to prison' (41). As the play progresses, the story takes on a life of its own. Believing the teenagers' story, the police find the man whose DNA Cathy and Mark planted on Adam's jumper. Ironically, it will turn out that Adam was not dead at all, and even the cover up was not based on the truth of events at all. As the play progresses, it is as if the boy they think they have killed refuses to be silent. Richard names his dog Adam, and Mark's pregnant mum plans to use the name for a baby boy.

Two of the characters in particular seem to oppose the pressure to stay silent. The first is Brian, whose first instinct is to tell someone what has happened. He is kept quiet, however, by the play's more forceful characters. The group's leaders, John Tate and Phil, physically intimidate Brian to shut him up. Through Brian, Kelly illustrates the psychological consequences of the cover up. Gradually, his mental health deteriorates, and he reverts to a childlike state. In the final wood scene he laughs and giggles hysterically at the idea of a 'game' to put a plastic bag over Adam's head. By the end of the play the audience hears he may be sectioned (admitted to a hospital because of severe mental illness), suggesting that he has completely lost his grip on reality.

In addition to Brian, Leah also resists silence. In some ways, she is the play's truth-teller, confronting events with an ethical and philosophical stance. When Danny and Lou reveal the news that 'they've found the man', Leah's instinct is to remind the group of the truth, 'I mean I'm not being fussy or anything, but the man that kidnapped Adam doesn't actually exist, does he?' (34). For much of the play, however, she is insufficiently sure of herself, and too much under the influence of the group's leaders to resist the cover up. In the first wood scene, she is easily silenced by John Tate's finger on her lips. When it becomes clear that the game Phil has shown Brian will have fatal consequences, Leah tries to suggest owning up to the crime, 'we can explain. We can talk. We can go through the whole thing and make them understand –' (58). Her outburst is in vain. At the end of the play, Leah's leaving is disconcerting. It is as if Leah evaporates, her voice silenced at the end of the play, and the rest of the teenagers are now desperately unhappy and trapped forever in a dreadful silence.

Discuss

1. Think about a time when you tried to cover up something you had done wrong. What kind of difficulties did it create and what kind of emotions did the experience bring out in you?

2. Imagine that Phil's plan had worked and the group had succeeded in covering up Adam's death. Would the teenagers have been right to tell no one?

Science, faith and philosophy

In Kelly's play, the teenagers are able to exploit a blind belief in the scientific 'evidence' provided by DNA. Alternative systems of belief, such as religion and philosophy, are also apparent to the audience, although their influence on events is not strong.

The symbolic resonances of Adam's story add a layer of religious allegory to *DNA*. The character's name and what happens to him are suggestive of both the first man, Adam, and of Jesus Christ, the son of God in the Christian faith. In the Bible, the first man was created by God, and lived with Eve in Paradise, until the couple was thrown out for committing the sin of disobedience. This is often referred to as 'the fall of Adam'. By choosing the name of Adam for the character that falls down the shaft, Kelly seems to be recalling and rewriting this Biblical story.

There are additional suggestions of Christian symbolism in the links that exist between Adam and Jesus Christ. Christians believe that Christ died for the sins of mankind. Nailed to and crucified on the cross, he is often depicted with wounds (called stigmata) through his hands and feet. With this in mind, it seems noteworthy that the gang stub out cigarettes on the soles of Adam's feet (22). In the Bible, the New Testament gospels report that Jesus Christ spent forty days in the wilderness. After his death, which Christians believe saved people from their sins, he is said to have come back to life before ascending to heaven. Adam too, who was bullied and teased by the group, survives in the wilderness, seems to die and comes back to life, only to die 'again' at the hands of the group. He describes being drawn towards the 'light', which again may have symbolic significance of God's light in heaven. There is no hint of an ascension to heaven however in *DNA*. Rather, Leah exclaims that 'they are naming the science lab after him, for god's sake' (55).

The murder of Adam suggests that the teenagers' world is ultimately one in which fear and self-interest are more powerful than religious faith. Although the characters rely on common religious references at key moments, they seem completely unaware of the symbolic significance of their language and behaviour. The first words spoken after Adam's monologue about his new life in the woods are Jan's, 'Jesus Christ' (55). Richard uses a facetious and dismissive tone when he reports that John Tate has joined the 'Jesus Army' (64). It seems that for the majority of characters in the world of *DNA*, religious belief and faith in a better world is simply not a serious possibility. Further, similarities between the way a religion works and the 'cult' of the gang are troubling. The teenagers place a blind faith in their leaders, and Leah even calls Phil a 'miracle worker', a term that can be associated with the descriptions of Jesus in the Bible making the blind see and the lame walk (47).

In *DNA*, the musings and actions of Leah arguably suggest a philosophical outlook as an alternative to a system of belief based on neither science nor religion. Leah asks questions, and thinks about the nature of existence. She is aware that the universe is huge, and that humankind is tiny, 'It's a big world Phil, a lot bigger than you' (46). In contrast, other members of the group are overcome by fatalism – the belief that humans are powerless – and that they are 'screwed' (12). In the field Leah asks Phil, 'Do you think it is possible to change things?' (42). Phil's answer, 'No', is fatalistic. Leah reaches a different conclusion, 'I do, Phil' (43). In the end, Leah makes an existential choice, spitting out Phil's sugar coated sweet, and deciding for herself to leave the group. Taking responsibility for herself, it is as if she has rejected group conformity, and the need to believe in a lie.

Things to do

Draw a picture of Adam, and label it with anything about the character and his story that suggests religious significance.

Discuss

1 Which has a stronger significance for the audience of *DNA*, religion or science?

2 How hopeful do you find *DNA*?

Characters

As with any play, the characters in *DNA* are not real, and they are far less complicated than real people. Nevertheless, they seem familiar, and are believable as young people. The following section considers the distinct qualities of each character, as well as their roles or functions in the play.

Adam

Mark's description of Adam as 'sort of hanging around', suggests a boy who goes along with his bullying out of a desperate need to be accepted (20). When Leah reminds Phil that they ate 'cheap ice cream' at his parties, and they 'used to take the piss', there is a hint that he is from a lower social class (58). Through Adam, Dennis Kelly illustrates the very worst aspects of human nature, as the audience learns of his dreadful bullying at the hands of the gang. Jan and Mark relate how he was punched in the face, had cigarettes stubbed out on his arms, hands, face and the soles of his feet, and was made to run across the motorway. Glimpses of Adam, 'laughing' and 'crying' at the same time elicit sympathy for the 'terrified' boy, even though they are narrated by his bullies (21). Mark's description of the 'shock' and 'fear' on Adam's face as the 'laughing' group throws stones at him is vivid, conjuring an image of a vulnerable, terror-struck boy, caught in a situation he is powerless to stop.

When he is found in the woods, the character of Adam gains a symbolic significance. The boy gives a spell binding account of what sounds like a near death experience and a rebirth, suggesting a religious allegory. His story resonates with those of the first man in the Christian bible and of Jesus Christ (see more commentary in the 'Themes' and 'Dramatic technique' sections). Kelly seems to be encouraging the audience to think of Adam as an innocent boy who has found an uncorrupted and primitive state away from the complex and corrupted ways humans live in society. As Cathy and Brian lead him off to put a plastic bag over his head, the murder of Adam represents the sacrifice of an individual to save the group.

Things to do

In small groups, improvise a scene where members of the group are at Adam's party and commenting on the food they have been given, the house, the music, etc. One of you is Adam. Try to make a joke of it all to be accepted by the group.

Discuss

1 Do you think that Adam is happier living in the woods than before?

2 Is Adam more or less human after he is found in the woods?

3 Look up and read the story of creation in the Bible (Genesis, Chapter 1, Verses 1–31). You can also read an account of Jesus in the wilderness (Matthew, Chapter 4, Verses 1–11). You will find some similarities and many differences between the stories of Kelly's Adam and Jesus. What do you think Kelly is trying to suggest by subtly alluding to the Bible stories?

4 How do *you* feel about Adam and what happened to him?

Brian

The character of Brian illustrates the bullying and manipulation by the group of its weaker members, and its damaging psychological effects.

He is an emotionally sensitive and relatively innocent boy who first appears '*crying*' with Richard and Cathy, bringing news of Adam's death (19). Although Brian is weak, and can be bullied into doing what the others say, his resistance to the cover up voices the group's alternative course of action, 'I think we should tell someone.'

Brian is the group member who is least willing and able to lie, and the one who is most coerced and bullied into doing so. He suffers severe psychological disturbances because he has lied, and feels bad and frightened. Through Brian, Kelly explores the effects of conscience, 'because I cry, they think I am telling the truth, but I'm crying because I'm lying and I feel terrible inside' (39). Not long after Phil has threatened that the group will kill him if he does not go to the police, Leah reveals that Brian is 'on medication' (47). Brian's line, 'I am brilliant at doing what people say', links thematically to the idea that group conformity can lead even to the murder of other human beings (60).

In the last wood scene, Brian acts as Adam's double. He seems to regress to a primitive state, as he imagines what Adam's new life is like. 'I love crawling', he says, 'Shall we eat earth?' (49–50). Like Adam, Brian seems also to have escaped from the pain and difficulties of living with other humans. However, his attempts to eat earth, his childish jabbering and his repeated outbursts of giggling and hysterical laughter, suggest that he is delusional. In the end, Brian seems to have lost all hold on reality rather than coming into closer contact with it. The audience's final glimpse of Brian, reported by Richard, is tragic. The boy now spends his time 'drooling and giggling', and staring at walls (64). Highly deranged, Brian is now likely to be sectioned and taken to a mental hospital.

> ### Things to do
>
> In a group, make still images of key moments for Brian. The images should show:
>
> 1 Brian arriving at the wood with Cathy and Richard.
> 2 Brian telling Jan and Mark he will not go to the police.
> 3 Phil threatening Brian that the group will kill him.

Cathy

Cathy is the character through whom Kelly most explores the disturbing idea that it is part of human nature to take pleasure in violence. She plays an important role in moving the plot forwards, planting the DNA evidence that frames the postman, and finding Adam in the woods.

When she first arrives with Richard and Brian, Kelly's stage directions specify that Cathy is '*grinning*'. She seems to get a thrill from the shocking events, finding the brutalizing of Adam 'mad', 'exciting' and, 'Better than ordinary life' (16). She stirs up trouble for Danny, with whom she has an ongoing feud, and undermines John Tate's leadership by claiming that Danny is 'on Richard's side' (17).

Cathy is cold and callous, showing no signs of guilt for the lives the group take or wreck. She thinks the Press interest in the disappearance of Adam is 'great', relishes the idea that she could be interviewed on television, and even considers asking for money (36). Over zealous in carrying out Phil's cover up, she sees nothing wrong in taking the 'initiative' in obtaining DNA from the postman.

As the play progresses, Cathy's love of violence becomes more pronounced. 'I used violence', she says, to get Adam out of the hedge: 'I threatened to gouge one of his eyes out' (50). As Brian states, 'She loves violence now' (51). When Cathy slaps him in the final wood scene, her threat is underlined by the sobering words, 'If you don't shut up, you'll be dead' (56). Unsurprisingly, Phil turns to Cathy to carry out the murder of Adam. She has become a ruthless killer. By the end of the play, the audience hears from Richard that Cathy is now 'running things' (64). The rumour that she has cut off a first year's finger suggests that her leadership will be the most terrifyingly violent of all.

Things to do

Imagine you are the costume designer for *DNA*. How does Cathy wear her school uniform? Draw a design for the character's costume, showing how it changes as the play progresses. Choose two other characters to do the same for. Gradually build up your portfolio as you think more about the characters in *DNA*.

Danny

Danny seems to be the most academic of the gang, and has ambitions to be a dentist: 'Dentists don't get mixed up in things. I've got a plan' (14). In some ways, with his concern for career and reputation, he brings the voice of adults into the dialogue. Throughout the play, Danny returns to this self-serving agenda, 'How am I gonna get references?' he whines in the second wood scene (35). As with other gang members, he is helpless in extreme circumstances. For all his ambitions, Danny is not quick-witted, and panics when under pressure. Asked by John Tate if he is on his side, Danny snaps, 'Yes, I'm on your side!' Moments later, he agrees to John Tate's plan to 'say nothing' (18). Danny is ultimately a passive member of the group who will do as he is told by the leader.

Throughout the play, Kelly creates comedy with Danny's obsessive concern with dentistry (see more under 'Humour and tone' below). There is something both comic and poignant, however, in the final scene in Richard's report that Danny hates his work experience at the dentists. 'Can't stand the cavities', he says. 'When they open their mouths it feels like you're going to fall in' (64). The description seems to have a metaphorical significance, with its resonance of the shaft into which Adam fell. It also hints of the lasting effects of the events on the teenagers' lives.

Things to do

Write Danny's end of term form tutor's report, commenting on his academic potential and his behaviour in class.

Jan and Mark

Jan and Mark are always seen together. They open each section of *DNA* with a tense and nervy duologue that takes place in a public street. Like a Chorus in Ancient Greek Drama, they help to move the story along, each time revealing that something new has happened. Kelly uses their scenes to create suspense, not revealing the details of what has happened until later. Typical of the group, Jan and Mark are unsure of what to do when in trouble, and always go to Phil for help, 'We need to talk to you' (12).

Kelly uses Jan and Mark to convey the cruelty of the taunting of Adam. Through their account the audience learns that for a 'half hour, forty minutes', the group was bullying and punching Adam, even stubbing out cigarettes on the soles of his feet (21–2). Both Mark and Jan try to absolve themselves of responsibility, repeating 'you know what he's like' as if Adam brought it on himself (20–22). Although some of their comments suggest that they knew he was 'scared', their frequent references to him as a 'nutter' dehumanize Adam, making him an outsider to the group, rather than a part of it (21–2).

In the final part of Mark's story, in which the audience listens in horror as he describes the stoning of Adam, the feral, brutal and pack-like behaviour of which the teenage gang is capable is made clear.

Things to do

Take on the role of a particular audience member. For example, you could be a fourteen-year-old schoolgirl or schoolboy, a mother or father of teenage children, a head teacher, or a grandparent. Imagine you are listening to Jan and Mark's account of the bullying of Adam for the first time. Vocalize your reactions to what you hear. The more seriously you do this the more effective it will be as an exercise. Now write a post for the theatre's website giving your response to this part of the play, including a comment on what (if anything) it tells us about young people today.

John Tate

Through John Tate's one scene, Kelly explores group dynamics, the exercise of authority, and the psychological effects of the cover up of Adam's death. John Tate is an important contrast to Phil, and during the course of the play John Tate's leadership wanes as Phil becomes more powerful.

The audience first sees John Tate in the first wood scene, trying to reassure Lou and Danny that 'everything's fine' (12–13). The frequent false starts and hesitations in his speech, 'No,

Lou, we're not ... it's not ... we're not ... nothing's ...', suggest insecurity. From the start, the character has to remind the others of his authority. 'Are you scared of anyone in this school?' he asks Lou. Her answer, 'You?' – a question rather than a statement – contains an element of uncertainty. When his ban on the word 'dead' is undermined by Richard, John Tate's response, 'Right, that's ... now I really am getting a little cross', sounds flustered and ineffectual (15). His vocabulary, slightly more formal than that of the other gang members, suggests that he may be from a more privileged background.

John Tate's fragile nature contrasts with his unsubtle leadership style. He calls Brian a 'crying little piece of filth', and as he walks menacingly towards him the audience sees that the tactics of the group leader have the potential to become physically brutal (19). The moment is broken when Leah and Phil arrive, and John Tate's vulnerable side is again revealed, 'I'm finding this all quite stressful', he complains, a line that foreshadows his subsequent withdrawal from the group (19). Like the other gang members, John Tate looks to Phil for help. His question, 'What do we do?' effectively concedes authority to the 'clever' boy (23).

After this scene, John Tate disappears from the action, but Leah subsequently reports that the character has 'lost it' and 'won't come out of his room' (32). In the final scene, Richard tells Phil that John Tate has 'joined the Jesus Army, spending his time singing in the shopping centre and handing out leaflets' (64). John Tate's religious conversion suggests an escape from the dreadful chain of events in which he has played a major role, or perhaps an attempt to propagate a more positive idea of human nature.

Discuss

1   John Tate is the only character in *DNA* to whom Kelly gives a surname. What might Kelly be trying to suggest?

> **2** John Tate likes to claim the credit for the status that the group enjoy, and seems to be behind the 'fear' and 'brutal terror' that Leah describes near the beginning of the play. To what extent do you think he can be held responsible for all the subsequent events?
>
> **3** Why do you think John Tate turns to religion?

Leah

Both talkative and curious, Leah seems driven to ask questions, about herself, about animals and humans, and about the world. Leah speculates on the qualities of chimps and bonobos, and the position of human kind in the universe. Aware of the vast world beyond Planet Earth, and the massive geological features of 'molten lava' and 'oceans of liquid nitrogen' she concludes that humans, and their odd behaviour, are the 'anomaly' (31). Loyal and generous, Leah's instinct is to defend Phil unselfishly by claiming joint responsibility: 'Whatever we did, we did, me and Phil, it wasn't just Phil . . . I am responsible as much as he' (18). Perhaps most importantly she acts as the group's conscience, asking questions about the morality of the group's behaviour, 'What have we done, Phil?' (32).

Another of Leah's roles in the play is to report events. Through her the audience learns that after fulfilling Phil's plan for the group, 'Everyone's happier' (32). Often, Leah guides the audience too, saying in her first scene that she is 'scared' and 'ashamed' of the 'brutal terror' that people are living with (12).

In spite of her capacity to think intelligently, Leah is very much part of the group. Often unsure and uncertain of herself, for much of the play Leah seems to look up to Phil, and to use him as a sounding board upon which to project her ideas and her anxieties. Although the audience does not see Leah participating in any bullying or cruelty directly, it is notable how violent her language can be, 'So kill me, Phil, call the police, lock me up, rip out my teeth with a pair of rusty pliers' (11). Leah's description of killing her dead pet, Jerry, with a screwdriver and hammer is also extremely unsettling.

Leah is a deeply sympathetic character, partly because of her humility and thoughtfulness, but also because of the personal struggle she undergoes during the play. Through Leah, Kelly suggests a veiled story of growing independence and courage. Shortly after the false arrest of the postman, Leah appears to have an epiphany. Her insight, 'if you change one thing you can change the world', suggests that it may be possible to break the cycle of behaviour in which the group is trapped. When Jan and Mark arrive with news that Brian has been found however, the limits to Leah's power are exposed. She fails in her attempt to convince the group that they can 'make them understand', and is powerless to intervene as Cathy takes Brian off with the plastic bag (58). It is not until Leah spits out the sweet that she has been given by Phil and storms off in her final scene that she finally seems to have escaped his influence.

Discuss

1 How would *DNA* be different if Leah was not in it?
2 Why do you think Leah stays so long?
3 Do you think she made the right decision by leaving?

Things to do

Write Leah's diary entry for three different points in the play. If you can, make these into a video diary that she makes in her bedroom at home.

Lou

With Lou's first word in the wood, 'Screwed', she establishes a tone of apprehension and fatalism (13). 'This is really serious', Lou pronounces, in spite of John Tate's attempts to calm the gang. Her continual references to the trouble the gang is in keep the tension levels high. In particular, her repeated line, 'We're screwed' becomes a darkly comic catchphrase, and her candid and open comments, 'He's shitting it', keep the tone of the play teetering on the absurd (35).

Kelly uses Lou to illustrate some typical characteristics of a lesser gang member. She is quick to blame others, calling Mark a 'dick' for framing the postman (39). Lacking a moral compass, she tends to be fickle, and follows the decisions of others. Both realistic and pragmatic, Lou does not challenge John Tate's ban on the word 'dead'. Like the others, she follows Phil's instructions in carrying out the cover up. She quickly forgets her comment, 'We're going to have to tell them', after Brian says he cannot face lying to the police. In the final scene, Richard reports that she is now Cathy's 'best friend' (64). Following the new leader, and 'playing a dangerous game', Lou has been sucked closer into a regime of terror. The fact that Richard feels 'sorry' for Lou however suggests to the audience a sympathetic response to the character.

Things to do

Working individually, half of the class should write a list of points in favour of the statement, 'Lou serves little function in *DNA'*. The other half of the class should write a list of points that disagree. Now join up with someone with the opposite view to debate the statement.

Phil

Most often seen away from the group with Leah, Phil is taciturn to the extreme. Enigmatic and often silent, he is nearly always seen eating or drinking some kind of junk food or snack. At first detached, he only becomes involved in the main action when John Tate turns to him for help believing him to be 'clever' (23). In response, Phil takes the decisive action of 'carefully' placing his Coke can down, in order to speak his first words – an extraordinary series of orders that give each of the troubled teenagers a clear role in the plan to fake Adam's disappearance. Although he says he is 'making it up' as he goes along, the plan reveals a breathtaking capacity to think ahead (25). Later in the play, Leah calls him a 'miracle-worker' (47). For a boy who is normally so silent, Phil is brilliant with language, and there are more examples of this as the play proceeds.

Phil is an extreme pragmatist, reacting and responding to events when it is needed, but otherwise choosing to remain impassive. In the field scenes, Leah's words, questions and actions have little effect on him. Even her attempt to strangle herself brings only a pause in eating his packet of crisps. The audience is likely to be puzzled by Leah's remark that she can talk to him because 'he can see the incredibly precious beauty and fragility of reality' (31). Her assessment towards the end of the play, 'Your brain is entirely waffle, single-mindedly waffle and maybe a bit of jam', seems more accurate. Phil's answer to Leah's question, 'If you change one thing you can change the world. Do you believe that?' is a blunt 'No.' This answer reveals Phil as a fatalist, a philosophical position that sees everything as inevitable, and humans as powerless. In the subsequent field scene he only shrugs in answer to her question, 'How do you feel?', almost as if he has no feelings, or certainly does not feel it is worthwhile voicing them.

As the play progresses, Phil's attempts to limit the damage the group has caused become more and more worrying. He bullies Brian into going to the police, threatening him with a cruel death if he refuses. 'You'll fall into the cold. Into the dark. You'll fall on

Adam's corpse and you'll rot together' (40). Phil's language is chilling and morbid, revealing a sinister capacity to manipulate and pressurize. In the final wood scene, Phil's actions illustrate Kelly's thematic concerns with the tensions between the rights of the individual and the needs of the group. His reasoning for the murder of Adam seems altruistic, 'Everyone is happier. What's more important; one person or everyone?' (58). Yet his justification, 'He's dead. Everyone thinks he's dead. What difference does it make?', comes across as callous.

By the end, Phil seems to have pulled off an astonishingly well executed cover up, but it is at the expense of the sanity of some group members, the corruption of others, the murder of a boy, and the false imprisonment for life of an innocent man. Phil's silence, so enigmatic and interesting to the audience at the beginning of the play, has become sinister, a sign that something is wrong. In her review in *The Times*, Libby Purves refers to Phil as a 'psychopathic ringleader', implying that a severe mental imbalance lies behind his criminal behaviour. His decrees to the group to 'Keep your mouths shut', and 'Don't say anything to anyone about this', have lead to a dreadful dystopia, in which the teenagers live a lie, and their mental health is destroyed. In the last field scene with Richard, the stage directions tell us that Phil spends his time '*staring at nothing*' (65). He has distanced himself from the group, and is unresponsive to Richard's plea, 'Come back to us' (63). Now more uncommunicative than ever, the character himself seems deeply unhappy. Without Leah and not eating, Phil seems locked into a silence of isolation.

Discuss

1 Do you think Phil plans his actions or reacts spontaneously?
2 Do you agree with Purves that Phil is a 'psychopathic ringleader'?
3 How do you feel about Phil in the final scene?

Things to do

1 Use the stage directions in *DNA* to find further clues to
   Phil's eating. Make a list of all the things that Phil eats
   throughout the play. How does he eat? Is he careful or
   sloppy with his food? During and after which events does
   Phil eat? Does he share food? Now make a picture to
   illustrate Phil's eating.

2 If you were an actor playing Phil, you would need to decide
   on what, if anything, is going on inside Phil's mind. Choose
   a scene with Leah, and decide what Phil is thinking in it.
   Act out the scene, and vocalize your thoughts. Now act it
   again without speaking.

Richard

Richard has a relatively high status within the group, and Kelly
uses the character to illustrate the rivalries and tensions within
it. The character has a certain dignified confidence, and does not
back down to John Tate. Although a little *'hesitantly'* he pulls
him up on his threats, 'You shouldn't threaten me, John' (17). In
spite of this, Richard is willing to accept Phil's authority. He
does as he is instructed, in spite of his objections to Brian, and
twice takes him off to fulfil Phil's orders. Like the other group
members, when things go wrong, Richard becomes helpless,
worried about going to prison, and needs Phil to suggest a way
forward.

In the final field scene Richard has in some respects taken
the place of Leah. Like Leah, he appears to be trying to get
Phil's attention, standing on his hands, 'See? See what I'm
doing? Can you see Phil?' (63). Like Leah, Richard brings news
of the other characters. Through him, we hear that Cathy has
cut off a first year's finger, that Jan and Mark are shoplifting,

and that Danny is hating his work experience at the dentist. This helps to create the sense of dystopia and futility that pervades the end of the play. Again like Leah, Richard opens wider perspectives, giving an invitation to stand back and reflect on human behaviour. Caught up in a 'big wind of fluff' on the way to the field Richard felt like an 'alien in a cloud', and sure that there is life on other planets (65).

Discuss

1 When he directed the play, Anthony Banks cast Richard as a good-looking, cool and popular teenager. If you were directing *DNA*, what would you look for in an actor to play Richard? How would you cast the other characters?

2 In the list of characters Kelly specifies that 'Names and genders are suggestions only, and can be changed to suit performers' (7). Why do you think that Kelly says that genders of the characters are suggestions only? What is he implying about the behaviour of girls and boys?

Things to do

1 Reallocate the parts so that they are read by the opposite gender. Do you think this makes any difference?

2 Match these adjectives with the character(s) you think they best describe.

thoughtful   taciturn   weak   certain   insecure   cruel

irresponsible   shallow   sensitive   intelligent   amoral

focused   self-deprecating   uncertain   strong

mature   lonely   immature   ruthless   masochistic

spontaneous   sadistic   curious   needy   dependent

reflective   loyal   childish   resourceful   conformist

questioning   naive   ambitious

Dramatic technique

Genre

In literature, the word genre refers to a specific type of writing, such as science fiction, fantasy or crime. There are also types of genre for music, TV and film. Not all plays fit neatly into one category of drama, and *DNA* seems to be a mix. In one sense, it is a *thriller*, because the plot has twists and turns, with unexpected events happening thick and fast. Kelly makes use of teasing cliffhanger endings to keep the audience involved in the plot. The play's focus on scientific evidence and DNA also give it a flavour of a contemporary *crime drama*, a genre that has been enduringly popular, particularly on television. *DNA* reverses the traditional focus of a crime drama by following the criminals rather than the detectives. The play is also a *tragedy*, a type of genre that goes back to the Ancient Greeks, in which the audience sees a sad story of human suffering, and feels pity and fear as a result. In a tragedy, it often seems that a chain of events is started that becomes inevitable, and that the power of fate rather than people is in control. At the same time, Kelly includes elements of *black comedy*, his teenage characters often making us laugh at the very moments when the action is most serious and deathly.

Plot and structure

Since Roman times, plays have often been divided into large divisions called acts. Each act is divided into smaller sections called scenes. Scenes can be longer or shorter in length depending on the dramatic action they contain. A play by William Shakespeare, for example, normally has five acts, which are divided into several shorter scenes. Together, acts and scenes give a play structure, helping to shape the action and narrative in a dramatically satisfying way.

Instead of using the traditional term acts, Dennis Kelly has divided *DNA* into four sections. Sections One, Two and Three each has four scenes, which make up a recurring pattern. Each first scene is set in a street, the second in a field, the third in a wood and the last in a field. The majority of the scenes are duologues (with two characters), but in the wood scenes the ensemble appears. In the last section the play's symmetry is broken, with only the street and one field scene. Because of the structural repetitions, it is almost as if the teenagers are caught in a cycle or pattern of behaviour from which it is difficult to break loose.

As well as the cyclical return of the play's locations, there is also a linear plot in *DNA* that hooks the audience in. Kelly has ordered the events of the play carefully, in a way that keeps us engrossed in the unfolding storyline. Key to this is the revelation of the events: throughout the action, Kelly skilfully chooses his moments to release information. The street scenes in particular function, according to Anthony Banks, as 'curtain raisers', enticing the audience into the play with partially revealed information that keeps the audience guessing, and wanting to see and hear more (see interview in 'Behind the Scenes').

Kelly employs a snowballing effect, each incident leading to the next, and becoming progressively harder for the teenagers to manage. The plot device is similar to that of an ancient tragedy, where Fate seems to have more control over what happens than the characters themselves. Of course, at a thematic level, the ideas of choices and of responsibility are exactly what

Kelly seems to be exploring. At any moment, the teenagers could tell an adult, and the more they cover up, the more they become responsible for the dreadful events.

As well as being aware of ancient dramatic structures, it is also useful to refer to the key devices that contemporary writers use. Many of these are described in Robert McKee's book, *Story* (1999), which analyses the close relationships in drama writing between plot, structure and character. In *DNA,* there is an *inciting incident* that takes place just before the action of the play begins. This is the bullying of Adam and his apparent death. The panic it generates in the young people enables the play to start dynamically. Already, the stakes are high, and the characters under pressure to deal with the awful accident. The plot or events of *DNA* therefore play an important part in the way that characters behave. The circumstances the teenagers are in force Phil to come up with a plan to cover up the crime. As McKee puts it, 'True CHARACTER is revealed in the choices a human being makes under pressure – the greater the pressure, the deeper the revelation, the truer the choice to the character's essential nature' (101). Whether the 'essential nature' of Phil, or any of the other teenagers, is cruel and murderous, or anything else, is of course also one of the play's central themes.

As the play progresses, there are *developments* in the plot. These happen when the police find the postman whose DNA is a match, and when Brian refuses to go to the police. One event seems to lead quickly to another, forcing the young people to take rash decisions. A major *complication* occurs when Adam is discovered still alive in the wood, piling pressure yet again on the characters to take yet more extreme measures to cover their tracks. Using a mixture of anticipation and surprise, Kelly keeps the audience involved. Not revealing that Adam is still alive means that they discover the truth along with the teenagers. Alert members of the audience may have guessed this beforehand, when Mark revealed in the preceding street scene that 'Cathy found him in the woods' (45). *Cliffhanger endings*, such as Leah's somber and ominous, 'Trouble now' at the end of section one, ensures the audience remain eager to see how the plot will pan out as the play continues (28). Eventually, events lead to the *climax* of the plot, when Phil instructs Cathy and Brian to stifle Adam with a plastic bag. At the end of the play, there is a brief final scene that provides a partial *resolution* as the audience hears what has happened to the gang members. Far from a happy ending however, the audience is left with the feeling that the incidents in the woods will forever haunt the lives of those it has touched.

DNA is a short play, packing in an enormous amount of action in approximately an hour's running time. Banks has described the story as 'irresistible . . . the events hurtle their way towards you thick and fast'. He also admires its variety, drawing attention to the way the field scenes between Leah and Phil provide changes in pace, giving the play both breathing spaces and texture: 'The juxtaposition of its two types of scenes gives you in one moment, the rush of a compelling thriller, and the next, the opportunity for deep contemplation' (Banks in AQA).

Discuss

1 Do the characters in *DNA* seem to be in control of their own actions?

2 Does Kelly suggest there are moments when they could have chosen to act differently?

Things to do

Use the section above to make a glossary of terminology to describe a play's plot and structure. As an example of how to do it, have a look at the 'Glossary' section in this book where some of the terms are already explained.

Humour and tone

Although *DNA* is in some respects a tragedy that deals with a chilling murder by a teenage gang, there is often a comic tone. Much of this humour comes from the characters of the teenagers as they struggle to deal with a situation that is beyond their control, and also from the tensions between them. At other moments, the tone of *DNA*'s comedy can be described as dark or black.

In the wood scene, as John Tate struggles to keep a lid on the group members' panic, Dennis Kelly uses the well-known comic device of undermining authority. Just as John Tate succeeds in banning the word 'dead', Richard arrives and breaks the silence the leader has enforced, with the very words he has banned, 'He's dead' (15). Humour often comes from character. Richard's response to the news about Adam, 'Dentists don't get mixed up in things', is funny, but comes from his sincere aspirations to qualify as a dentist (14). His interjection into Phil's instructions on the fat Caucasian male with a postman's uniform, 'What were his teeth like?' brings back the joke, which runs throughout the play (25). Much of this humour tends to make the audience feel sympathetic to the characters.

There is often comedy at unexpected points in the play. Even after Adam has been found, and delivers his extraordinary monologue, Kelly uses comic relief to break a tense moment. Brian bursts out with, 'I love this! This is great! Mates!' (56). The humour is often related or closely linked to a serious event or theme in the play: as Brian becomes more damaged, not all of the laughter that the character elicits is entirely comfortable. Brian's delight may make the audience laugh, but it is 'mates' who have pressured him into deceiving the police and who will now take advantage of his mentally unbalanced state to trick him into murdering Adam. The mood can also change suddenly in *DNA*. Following Brian's hysterical suggestion, 'Shall we hold hands?' Cathy slaps him to shut him up, an act that instantly and dramatically changes the tone (51).

The fine lines between laughter, disapproval and uncertainty become a dilemma for audience members. Some moments seem strange and unsettling, and 'darkly comic', rather than laugh out loud funny. Laughter itself relates to the thematic concerns of the play, as Kelly explores the way the teenagers laugh at things that are cruel or distressing. One of the clearest examples of this is in Mark's recollection of the teenagers throwing stones at Adam, and laughing.

> So we're all peggin then. Laughing. And his face, it's just making you laugh harder and harder, and they're getting nearer and nearer. And one hits his head. And the shock on his face is so ... funny ... (23)

This is one of the most serious and distressing moments of the play, reminding the audience of the ways that an individual is marginalized and dehumanized through the laughter of the group.

It is also worth considering if in writing this play for young people Kelly has captured a type of humour and range of tones that are specifically youthful. Responses from adults to the Connections plays at the National Theatre have emphasized their youthful sensibilities. Reviewer Rachel Halliburton, writing on Connections' productions *Burn/ Citizenship/ Chatroom*, thought that in the plays' scripting writers had been able to release 'a more honest register of emotions' and 'greater playfulness' (Halliburton 2006). Similarly, Sheridan Morley commented that the writers had 'plugged themselves into the complex rhythms of colloquial teenage speech and attitude' (Morley 2006). Banks, who as head of the Connections project had been closely involved in the development of *Citizenship*, identified its special youthful quality as 'flippancy', a style and tone that made the play 'immediately accessible' to its young audiences (Banks 2008).

Discuss

1   One response to Leah's description of the highly
    sexualized behaviour of bonobo monkeys might be
    laughter. They're 'Sex mad', she tells us, 'Sex, sex, sex,
    sex, sex, sex, sex, sex, sex, constant sex' (27). Is there a
    darkness underneath this description? What might Kelly
    be suggesting about human nature?

2   Do you think the humour in *DNA* is specifically youthful?
    Why? / Why not? Find examples from the text to support
    your ideas.

Language and dialogue

Kelly's style is exciting, drawing the reader or audience into a
dynamic and fast-paced story, while leaving much to fuel the
imagination. In many of the scenes the characters' speeches
overlap, creating a tense, excited atmosphere. Some scenes are
slower in pace, and contain long, significant silences. These
pauses and silences can tell you as much about characters and
significant moments as what they actually say. His characters
tend to speak in a simple, direct style, which is designed to
capture the language and rhythms of 'real' or 'natural' speech.
The voices sound youthful, due to the colloquial language, and
because of the relative unsophistication of vocabulary.

Although Kelly's dialogue looks simple on the surface, it is
packed with complexities and subtexts that will give you a lot
to explore. In a way, he seems to leave 'gaps' in the story or
dialogue, which he invites the audience to fill in using their
own ideas. In order to demonstrate Kelly's technique with
language, form and structure (focusing on AO2 in your
examination), I want to give you a close reading of the
beginning of the play. Although the first scene is short, and in
performance only a few moments long, Kelly sets up the story,
introduces characters and themes, creates a tense and thrilling

atmosphere, and sets an intense tone that teeters on the edge of humour. Reread it aloud now before you continue.

The first word of the play is 'Dead?' This is a highly dramatic start. A shocking event has occurred, but it is not revealed to whom or what is being referred. Incredulous, Jan repeatedly questions Mark's information, and he has to work hard to get her to believe it. The gravity of his tone is marked, many of his speeches finishing with a definite full stop, 'No mistake.' 'Not a joke.' This contrasts with the way Jan's sentences are often unpunctuated, as she tries to take in and process what Mark is saying. A feature of *DNA* is the very high stakes with which the action is played. Here, the pace is fast, a sense of urgency generated with fragmented sentences, or one word lines of speech, as the characters speak over each other. Once Mark has persuaded Jan of the death, and the information begins to sink in, her shocked, repeated single word responses, 'Oh' and 'God' seem to bring symbolic significance to the situation, a layer of religious reference which will become pronounced when Adam is found in the woods.

The scene finishes as it started, with a question, 'What are we going to do?' Not only does Kelly hook in the audience with this question, he links plot and character, suggesting the teenagers' helplessness at dealing with the unfolding events. As the play's 2012 director Anthony Banks describes, 'The street scenes are like little curtain raiser scenes.' By the end of the scene, the audience is ready for more.

Things to do

Choose a section of the text where the dialogue is fast-paced and the teenagers speak over each other. Can you get the timing right when you read it in a pair or group? How does learning the dialogue help? Using this book's analysis of the opening scene to guide you, write an analysis of the language and dialogue, linking your points to character, theme and structure.

Another key feature of Kelly's dialogue is the way it seems to replicate the false starts, repetitions, hesitations and self-corrections that people use in real speech. This is very apparent in Leah's speeches in particular. Take a look at this passage from the first field scene where she is speaking to Phil about having friends:

So don't, because you haven't either, I mean it's not like you're, you know, Mr, you know, popular, you know, you haven't, you know, you haven't, you know, you haven't, but that's different, isn't it, I mean it is, it is, don't say it isn't, really, don't, you'll just embarrass us both because it is different, it's different because it doesn't matter to you. Does it. Sitting there. Sitting there. Sitting there, all . . . all . . . (11)

Notice that Leah repeatedly starts a sentence then changes course, her speech becoming a mass of false beginnings and hesitations. Her sentences are often not finished at all, and leave the audience to fill in the gaps. This would be a hard speech to learn as an actor, but each word is important, because it suggests something about Leah's character, her relationship with Phil, and the difficulties she is having in articulating her meaning.

Things to do

1 Underline and identify any features in Leah's speech that sound 'real'. Do you think everyone speaks like this, or is it only Leah?

2 Investigate how lifelike Kelly's dialogue is. Listen to your friends speaking. Do they speak like Kelly's characters? What is similar or different? What does listening to real speech tell you: (a) about the way Kelly constructs

his teenagers' dialogue; and (b) about the differences
between real speech and dramatic dialogue?

3 Do your own close reading of passages from *DNA*. See if
you can comment on style of language (eg. colloquial,
poetic, fragmented, slow paced); sentence length and
structure (eg. overlapping, fragmented); tone (humorous,
anxious); punctuation, etc. Try to shape and structure your
close reading into two paragraphs that comment on the
characters and the situations they are in. (It is usually best
to link the details of language use to the topic you will be
asked to write about in an examination.)

Monologues

There are special, set pieces in *DNA* in which only one character
speaks at length. Mark's gripping and horrific account of the
dreadful taunting of Adam draws the audience in, as the incident
he recounts becomes more and more shocking. Adam's
monologue, where he recounts his life since falling through the
grille, is both fascinating and beautiful, providing the audience
with a window into the boy's emotional and physical 'rebirth'.
Both these monologues create serious interludes, texturing the
high-energy passages and the teenagers' panicky banter with
spellbindingly serious and moving tones.

Adam's monologue in particular is rich in symbolic
significance, and Kelly has used many techniques to poetically
heighten it. In the monologue, Adam recounts a long time
spent crawling in the dark. His speech is fragmented and jerky,
an effect that Kelly achieves by sometimes placing only one
word on a line, such as 'dark' and 'things'. The word 'dark' is
repeated several times, and the effect is to create a sense of
Adam's disorientation and confusion when he was crawling
underground (53–4). Yet he also says that 'the dark was my

fear' that wrapped him 'Like a soft blanket', a strangely warm and reassuring simile. It is possible to read this account as an extended metaphor of a re-birth, as if the dark tunnel is a womb, the blood on Adam's head the amniotic fluid, and his emergence into light his coming into the world.

Once in the 'light', the metaphors of birth and infantilism continue. Full of wonder, the boy recalls feeling 'sad', then 'new' and 'happy', until it was 'dark' again (54). Adam also dwells on the word 'light', as if now living a primitive or animal like existence in response to day and night. 'Light' may also carry a further religious significance, symbolic of God's heavenly light. The speech has a profound effect on both the audience and the teenagers. Jan is the first to respond, 'Jesus Christ', with an expression that references the Christian son of God (55). It is as if Adam, the first man in the Bible, has been reborn (see further commentary in 'Themes' section).

Things to do

Imagine you are an actor, preparing the part of Adam. Decide what are the most important words and images in his monologue. Imagine yourself doing what Adam describes in the monologue, and feeling what he is feeling. Now act the whole speech out to a partner, or if you are feeling brave, to the whole class.

Set and design

Dennis Kelly does not specify a town where the action of *DNA* takes place, and there is very little naturalistic detail. This lack of specific place names suggests that the play could take place in any street, any field and any wood.

Each setting however does have a distinctive atmosphere. A street is a busy public space, where other people might overhear, and can also give a sense of business and movement. A field is a much more open space, surrounded by nature, where the pace tends to be slower, and there is time to think. A wood can be dark, shadowy or dangerous, a place to hide or get lost. Many fairy tales happen in woods, and often bad things happen to children. In William Golding's novel, *The Lord of the Flies*, the boys are afraid of the jungle, and think a 'beast' might live there. Both the field and the wood are places away from adults, where the teenagers can go to be with each other and discover things for themselves.

Discuss

1 Why has Dennis Kelly chosen these locations?
2 Why do certain actions happen in certain places?
3 Why do you think Kelly did not set the scenes anywhere except the wood, street and field?

Things to do

Use a sheet of sugar paper to make a map of the play with the most important places and incidents plotted on to it. Use different colours for the wood, the street and the field. See if you can take over a display board, a classroom wall, or even a corridor. Find and add photographs, including locations such as the school, the Asda, and the police station.

When a play is staged, the settings of the play are turned into a design for the stage. The *settings* of field, street and wood become the *set*, which recreates these places for the theatre. The challenge of staging *DNA* is to convey the three different locations on one stage without slowing the action down. Of course, this can be done with the help of sound effects or music, and by creating the right mood and atmosphere for each piece. 'You don't need a real field or a real forest', Anthony Banks told me when I interviewed him for this guide. Here I quote Banks' description of his design and set for *DNA* at length, as it is full of rich detail about the play and the choices made for the touring production.

MI: As well as directing *DNA* in 2012 you also designed it. Can you tell me about the choices that you made?

AB: Plastic is at the centre of the design concept. It seemed that on some level, the play is about what is man made and what is of the earth and natural. The set is plastic, the actors are real! You could do two lists, the sky, the land, the trees, human beings. On the other list you've got authority, the state, the police. Plastic bags are used by the young criminals in order not to get their DNA on the jumper, but they're also used by the police in the form of gloves when they're going about looking for clues in the woods. I thought we'd make the whole thing out of plastic, including the floor, which was a QR code. I drew a version of it myself, scanned it into the computer and replicated it hundreds of times. It looked like leaves in the forest. I took photos of leaves, printed them out on acetate, and that became the gobos that the lighting designer used to project the leaves in the forest. So you could go from squares to natural forms.

Similarly with the back wall of the set, which was strips of translucent plastic, to look like a butcher's curtain that made you think of abattoirs or mortuaries. With trees, I took lots of photos of trees with some movement, and they were projected onto the curtain. The actors came through the slits of the curtain as if coming from the forest. It also became urban landscapes, sometimes the bleeding lights of cars for the street scenes. We set all the street scenes in a different place. One was on a train. The video designer filmed a train journey that became the backdrop, so that it looked as if the actors were on different trains having the conversation on their phones. In the field, we had different sizes of plastic grass. The grass was plastic but it looked real. Each time you saw the field, it was in a different part of the stage. The final one was a complete piece of grass that stretched the whole width of the field.

Things to do

1 Draw a picture and label the different elements of the 2012 set design for *DNA* that Banks describes above. Include as many details as possible.

2 Imagine there is going to be a new production of *DNA* in your school. As the play's designer, draw sketches for the design. Include details of colour, the kinds of materials you would use, and how the set would be made. Present your design to the class.

3 Imagine you are the sound designer for the new production. You have decided to play bursts of music in between the scenes. Choose your tracks and make your playlist, thinking carefully about the mood you would want to create for each scene. Play some of your choices to the class and explain them.

Critical reception and other commentaries

Critical reception

When a play is performed at the theatre, it will often be reviewed for newspapers and websites. Reviewers, also called critics, will come to see the play and write up a review in order to inform readers of its content and qualities. Often, good reviews will encourage more people to come and see the play, whereas bad ones can make people stay away. Some audience members prefer not to read reviews so that they can make their own minds up without being influenced.

How a play is reviewed or received is often referred to as the critical reception. It is useful to know about because it can tell us a lot about the context in which a play was written and performed, and what the reviewers thought was important at the time. Reviews can also give interesting and alternative insights into the play that can supplement – but not replace – your own personal response.

Here, I explore the critical reception of *DNA*'s 2008 and 2012 productions.

Many reviews praised Dennis Kelly's skills as a playwright. David Benedict commented that Kelly's control of his 'terrified characters is masterly', and his handling of language, 'equally exciting'. He found 'a lethal comic absurdity to his bald, repetitive dialogue' (2008). In 2012, Lyn Gardner also admired Kelly's 'jet-black comedy', as well as a plot that 'cleverly piles on the twists' (2012). Louise Lewis found Kelly's dialogue 'fast-paced and funny' (2012).

A. S. H. Smith commented on Kelly's 'black comedy', and the difficulty it caused audiences 'to know when to laugh' and when laughing was 'acceptable' (2012). The play's young audience, he observed, on the night he saw the show, laughed abundantly. Smith's comments raise the issue of whether the play captures something in its tone that is specifically youthful and appealing to young audiences.

Comments on the skill of the actors reveal interesting interpretations of the character of Leah. According to Billington, she was played by Ruby Bentall as an 'unstoppable chatterbox' (2008). Admiring the way 'Bentall unshowily delineates every single idea and separate change of thought', Benedict described Leah as 'Phil's earnestly talkative, forever-questioning pal Lea (sic)' (2008). When the part was played by Leah Brotherhead in 2012, Gardner found the actress 'moving and desperately funny as the needy Lea (sic), whose verbal squits disguise a yearning need to be loved' (2012). Smith felt that Leah is 'evidently in love' with Phil, and as such is his 'most obvious victim' (2012). These responses suggest not only the actresses' skill, but also the sympathy that the character of Leah elicited. Of course, you can make your own mind up about the degree to which she is Phil's 'victim'. Certainly, the comments made by the play's writer, director and actors (see interviews below in 'Behind the Scenes') suggest a more mutually beneficial relationship.

The reviews of *DNA* reveal the concerns over teenage behaviour that I identified above in the 'Contexts' section. It is striking how many of the reviews of both productions saw the play as an updated version of William Golding's novel *Lord of the Flies*, particularly with regard to its depiction of a world where adults are distant creatures. Benedict noted the absence of adult characters: 'Kelly's "DNA" banishes adults altogether. Authority figures – police, teachers, parents – exist offstage solely as people to be controlled, circumvented and deceived' (2008).

Many reviewers commented on how Kelly's portrayal of teenage behaviour sheds light on human nature, seeing this theme in both Golding's novel and Kelly's play. Gardner noted the way that *DNA* exposes how 'self-interest, peer pressure and an inability to really connect and empathise with others leads to a creeping corruption' (2012). Smith picked out its exploration of 'herd mentality and nature's brute wiring' (2012). Lewis observed how Kelly 'probes the very nature of humans themselves' through his depiction of teenage behaviour. She concluded, 'In Kelly's reality, we are certainly closer to the chimpanzees than hippy loving bonobos' (2012). Again, it would be possible to challenge this view, and it is a point that Kelly himself addresses in my interview with him below ('Behind the Scenes'). Michael Billington's praise for Kelly's understanding of 'the dynamics of group panic' suggests Kelly's emphasis on the way the teenagers deal with the situation that they find themselves in rather than their violent behaviour (2008).

Reviewers often picked out the character of Phil, many interpreting him as dangerously unbalanced. Billington noted the 'pathological self-control of Sam Crane's schoolboy superman' (2008). Libby Purves called him a 'detached almost psychopathic ringleader' (2012). The sentiment is echoed by Smith: 'Phil is, to all intents (and certainly all purposes), a psychopath' (2012). Similarly, to Gardner, Phil was 'an eccentric teenage criminal mastermind who may be a genius or a psychopath' (2012). Gardner noted James Alexandrou's 'creepily hilarious' portrayal of Phil as 'the almost electively mute schoolboy superman who obsessively stuffs his face with junk food as if trying to fill a black hole deep inside of himself'. Benedict framed Phil as a more familiar type of teenager, 'bright but nerdy Phil (intense, creepily cool Sam Crane)' (2008). All these critical responses to the character of Phil demonstrate how fascinating and central to the play he is. They also, it can be argued, reflect a concern amongst adults with the nature and behaviour of teenagers.

Things to do

Highlight at least six of the quotations that I have included from the reviews. Say whether you agree or disagree with them and why. Make a simple table that includes the quotations and your own opinions.

Here is a longer extract from the review by Libby Purves in *The Times* of the 2012 production. In common with many of the other reviews of *DNA*, it contains much praise for Kelly's writing and the actors' performances. Many of the phrases that Purves uses also suggests an anxious response to the play's representation of teenagers.

'I can't get mixed up in this, I'm gonna be a dentist!' shouts Danny (Tom Clegg). It's one of the few laughs in this riveting portrait of teenage brutality. He is one of a gang of teenagers who did a terrible thing. At this moment we don't know what. Soon the horror will loom over the rest of Hull Truck's tight, sparely set production.

Dennis Kelly's play was first written for The National Theatre's youth *Connections* festival, and adopted as a school text: this is its first national tour and brilliant. From the detached psychopathic ringleader (James Alexandrou) to the anxious twittering Leah (Leah Brotherhead) all the cast convince utterly, both as individuals and as a group whose interdependence trumps conscience.

The story is too gripping to spoil, but begins with an account of bullying which spun out of control. It is Richard (George Brockbanks) who relates it in a stunning monologue, others muttering alongside. Having recently seen Edward Bond's *Saved* with its famous baby-stoning scene, woefully unsupported by and psychological truth, it was salutary to have it expressed so believably. 'He was like, pretending, he was laffing. At first . . . we took it a bit far . . . stubbed out cigarettes on him . . . he is laffing, and crying . . . the fear on his face, you had to laugh . . .' Later the childlike terror: 'There'll be inquiries, police, mourning, a service . . . if we all keep our mouths shut it will be all right.'

Led by the taciturn Phil, who combines moral nullity with cop-drama sophistication, a cover story is devised to harness adult paranoia about paedophiles. The title refers to that cunning, but also to Leah's account of a documentary about how aggressive chimps differ from peaceable bonobos only by a speck of DNA. Without hammering it, the point is made that within humanity lies an instinct to torment and bait.

Kelly, like Graham Greene in *Brighton Rock,* combines enormous moral themes with painfully close understanding of the way a child's cruel irresponsibility can exist alongside an adolescent's power to hurt. They are not played as damaged, neglected children, but sport socially variable accents and refer to bygone birthday parties. There are two terrifying twists, but almost more chilling is the way that, childishly, the girls observe that the counselling, memorial and TV attention have improved the school's morale. 'It's like, grief is making them happy.'

PURVES 2012

Discuss

1 What words and phrases does Purves use to describe the writing and performances?

2 What words and phrases describe the characters' behaviour and how it illustrates human nature?

3 What different words does she use to describe the age of the characters in *DNA*? Why do you think she chooses them?

4 What do you think Purves means by her description of the characters as 'a group whose interdependence trumps conscience'?

5 How could you argue against her view of Phil?

Arts Council assessment

Theatre critics are not the only people who pass judgement on a piece of theatre. Assessments are also made by producers and funders. Some arts companies receive a grant from Arts Council England, an organization that decides how to spend public money on the arts. This was the case for the 2012 *DNA* tour, where Hull Truck theatre company received money from the Arts Council to make it. For the assessor from the Arts Council, who was sent to report on the artistic quality of the work, *DNA* was 'a coruscating and thought-provoking play of ideas', 'beautifully clear and coherent', with 'excellent production values' (Arts Council England). Like the reviewers, *DNA*'s assessor also commented on the play's portrayal of human nature and young people: 'The play poses so many moral questions about identity, leadership, group pressure, and issues of what is good and what is evil ... It is so good to see a play of ideas about who we are and how our young people are confronting the world.' The play's reception by its young audiences and the effect that the play was having on them was also noted: 'The audience appeared riveted throughout the performance, with some laughter at the dark humour ... It was as if they were collectively engrossed and struggling with the ideas and implications of what we were seeing.'

Discuss

1 Would you fund a production of *DNA* if you had the money? Why/ why not?

2 What kind of theatre would you fund if you had the money? Would you choose to give money to, for example, new plays about Britain today, productions of classics such as Shakespeare, musical shows, drama festivals, or projects where all kinds of ordinary people can get involved? Or something else? Why?

Other commentaries

Since the 2000s, as I indicated in the 'Contexts' section, there has been a flourishing of interest in drama for young people. This was partly caused by the New Labour government's policies, which provided more money for theatre. Under New Labour, Arts Council England prioritized funds for theatre for children and young people. Young people became more visible and audible in mainstream theatre, and higher *production values* were brought to theatre for young people – more time and money was spent on polishing a finished product for a paying audience.

Here, Suzy Graham Adriani, who founded Connections in 1995, describes the state of theatre for young people in the 1990s:

> Young people weren't well served. We had the adult canon of work: huge, brilliant, then the world of literature for teenagers that was great, but theatre wasn't paying attention to them. There was theatre for young people, TIE [Theatre in Education], but nobody was writing theatre for young people to perform themselves.

> GRAHAM ADRIANI in Lane

The Connections programme has indeed created a vast body of plays that have been performed by hundreds of young people every year. It has also sent the published plays to school libraries. Yet it is possible to challenge the ways that the programme chooses to work with young people. Connections plays are written by adult writers, rather than by young people themselves. It is interesting to speculate whether this causes the plays to reflect adults' concerns and views, rather than those of young people themselves. Would teenagers write and produce different plays? Further, when the Connections plays have been professionally staged at the National Theatre (NT), members of the youth theatres that had taken part in the festival were not asked to perform. Instead, professional actors were cast. Perhaps these decisions make for a 'better product', rather than aim to bring even better ways of participating and empowerment for young people.

Lane discusses the Connections programme in *Contemporary British Drama*, and quotes from his interview with Paul Miller, the director of the first professional production of *DNA* at the NT:

> Although the commissions could be accused of being adult commentaries on the experiences of young people as they see them, the plays escape from being patronizing because they deal with complex experiences from young people's

perspectives. They remain at the centre of the play's stories, and manage to 'tackle moral issues without being moralising. . .The world is presented as experienced from a young person's point of view; it is the same material world we inhabit as adults, but articulated differently'.

LANE, 151

Discuss

1 Do you agree that *DNA* gives a young person's perspective?
2 Does the play deal with young people's concerns?
3 How is theatre produced professionally in a mainstream theatre different from the plays you do in school? Is it 'better'?

Things to do

Imagine that you have been given funding to form a young person's theatre company. What kind of plays would you want to put on? What kind of issues would they deal with? Give your theatre company a name. Now decide *what* your plays will be about, *where* they will be performed, and *who* will write and perform them.

Related work

Other work by Dennis Kelly

Dennis Kelly is a prolific writer who has written many dramas and comedies for theatre and TV. His work is very varied indeed. Here is a selection of some of his works that make useful comparisons or contrasts with *DNA*.

Debris, Theatre 503, 2004.

Taking Care of Baby, Hampstead Theatre, 2007.

Orphans, Traverse Theatre Edinburgh, 2009.

Our Teacher's a Troll, Mull Theatre, Druimfin, 2009.

Matilda, Royal Shakespeare Company, Stratford-upon-Avon and West End, 2010–.

Utopia, Channel 4, 2013–14.

These works share some of the themes and concerns of *DNA*. Often, there are young characters who have been neglected by or isolated from adults, and there are violent incidents that are part of a thrilling or disturbing chain of events. Violence, and coping with its aftermath, is a preoccupation in Kelly's work that reflects his concern with the extremes of human nature and behaviour. Often, plots revolve around an inciting incident, or a mystery or event about whose truth the audience cannot be sure.

In *Orphans,* the audience is hooked in by the arrival of Liam at the house of his sister, Helen, and brother-in-law Danny. Liam is covered in blood, and he tells them it is from a wounded man he 'found' in the street. Knowing that Liam has been in trouble before for beating people up, Helen and Danny have to decide whether to involve the police. In this abridged passage, Helen puts pressure on Danny to give Liam an alibi by acting as if she is calling the police:

Beat.   She goes over to the phone, picks it up.

Danny   What are you doing?

. . .

Helen   I'm not being dramatic I'm just calling the police and turning my only brother in to the custody of the law.

Liam   Er, Hels?

Helen   Because we either do something or we don't
   Danny . . . there's having a family or not having a
   family, there's us and them, protect or not.
   . . .
   You don't go out after dark any more. You cross the street
   when you see a group of lads. You sit in the bottom deck
   of the bus and you stop talking when there are boys
   around. I need to know if you are a coward.
Beat
   I hate living here, are we going to live here forever? I'm
   not frightened of doing things for my family. Liam
   would die for his family. He would die for us, lay down
   his life for Shane, he would willingly stop breathing to
   save you.
Danny   I'm not frightened of doing things for my family
   either.
Helen   Are you going to help?
   Are you going to help?
   Are you going to –
Danny   Yeah.

KELLY 2013, 158–9

Discuss

1 How does Helen put pressure on her husband to protect
   her brother?

2 How do characters in *DNA* and *Orphans* share attitudes
   to crime?

Kelly's plays for children and families were written for
different audiences and purposes from *DNA*. Yet they have
some similar concerns. Both *Our Teacher's a Troll* and *Matilda*,
which Kelly adapted from Roald Dahl's children's book, are
concerned with power relationships, cruelty, bad behaviour,

and human nature. This is the speech given near the end of *Our Teacher's a Troll* by the dreadful child-eating troll who has taken over Sean and Holly's school:

> I am, indeed, a Troll. And as of a Troll, I am a Troll and the most Trollerous in nature. And it is in my most high and glorious nature to the bite the heads off the naughty childeains and to crunch and to crunch and to eat and to crinch, for this is what I was creationed to do. But I can see that you, a child and a childerain as well, and the other ones, the childs and the childers, the kids and brats and boodlums alike, have unto you a nature of your own, and – though not as glorious as mine – are in fact of a nature. And it is in your naturedness to commit acts of naughtiness. You just cannot help it. So. I have decided, in my wisdom of the infinatinity, to make a decree that if you shall maketh of the attempt to try not to be and therefore not to commit acts of naughtiness, I shall try and therefore to make of the attempt to not be biting the heads off any more of the childerains with the crunching and the crinching and the eating no more. No more I say!

KELLY 2013

Discuss

What thematic similarities do you find in this speech with *DNA*? It will help in particular to think of Leah's speech about chimps and bonobos.

Related work by other writers

In the interview I did with Dennis Kelly for this guide he told me that *Lord of the Flies* (1954) by William Golding was a big influence on all of his work. The novel is about a group of schoolboys who have to fend for themselves when they are marooned on a desert island after a plane crash. In *Lord of the Flies,* Golding explores human nature, and the tensions between the individual and the group. Different leaders emerge, hierarchies develop, and fear drives the boys' behaviour. *Lord of the Flies* contains a range of memorable characters, including the responsible choir boy Ralph, the wild and warlike Jack, and the bespectacled, overweight working class boy Piggy.

Another novel that has influenced Kelly is *I'm the King of the Castle* (1970) by Susan Hill. The novel concerns a young boy, Charles Kingshaw, who moves to a large house so that his mother can work there as a housekeeper. The boy is cruelly and unfairly bullied by the owner's son. As in *DNA,* Hill explores a childhood world where children are distant and isolated from adults. Reading these novels would give you an insight into the adultless world that Kelly explores in *DNA.* They would also be interesting and enjoyable reads in their own right.

Other plays for or about young people

As I mentioned in the 'Contexts' section, many plays were written and produced for and about young people in the 2000s. The Connections series at the National Theatre, of which *DNA* is one, was written especially for young people to perform. In 2006, the year before *DNA* was produced, Mark Ravenhill's *Citizenship*, Deborah Gearing's *Burn*, and Enda Walsh's *Chatroom* were produced professionally at the National Theatre. Outside the Connections programme, plays such as Leo Butler's *Redundant* (2001), Roy Williams' *Fall Out* (2003) and *Joe Guy* (2007), and Tanika Gupta's *White Boy* (2008) were also about young people. They portrayed shocking teenage behaviour, the grim social problems that young people can face, racist bullying and gang life. Often these plays, presented the young people in a realistic way, capturing the language and rhythms of young people's speech.

The following is a short extract from Leo Butler's *Redundant*, which portrays the life of Lucy, a Sheffield seventeen-year-old who lives in a council flat. Here, she is talking to Darren, another seventeen-year-old.

Lucy   You're funny you.
Pause.
    Not too bored are yer?
Darren   I'm not bored.
Lucy   No, but once yer've lived 'ere a bit. Starin' at the box all day.
She sits next to **Darren**.
Lucy   I like yer trainers. They new?
Darren   Yeah.
Lucy   Where d'yer get 'em?
Darren   Town.

BUTLER 2001, 7

This is a brief glimpse into the world that Butler has created, but it gives an idea of the concerns of his characters and the way they express themselves. Notice how naturalistic the dialogue is, as Butler seems to capture the accent and speech patterns of the voices of these Yorkshire teenagers.

Enda Walsh's *Chatroom* takes a very different approach to portraying young characters. The play presents a group of teenagers who meet in an internet chatroom to share their lives and problems. The following extract presents Eva and William complaining about the ways in which teenagers are viewed by adults.

William   A teenager is a sub-person . . . This hormonal mess. A boy-man, a girl-woman. We're like a bad experiment.
. . .
Eva   . . . It's a joke 'cause those adults who have lived through these years remember them with complete and utter embarrassment . . . By fifteen you're realized that

the individual doesn't mean shit and the average
teenager is seen as the big embarrassing joke.

William   We're all just folded up neatly and placed into a
box marked 'The Awkward Years'. We're trapped in the
cliché by those who have already lived though the cliché.

Shell Connections 2015, 186–7

These teenagers are speaking fluently, generally using standard
English, but with some colloquial speech. They are intelligent
and articulate, more than capable of reflecting and reaching
their own conclusions about the way adults think of them.

Discuss

1 How do the above extracts portray teenagers?

2 How have the writers used language and dialogue to
create particular dramatic effects?'

3 How are these teenage voices similar or different to
those in *DNA*?

Glossary of dramatic terms

Action   The action of a play consists of the events that the characters
take part in during the play.

Allegory   A story that can be read in more than one way or on
different levels.

Audience   An audience refers to a group of individuals who come to
see a play. In this book I have often used 'audience members' or
'audiences'. No two audience members and no two audiences are ever
the same.

Blocking   Blocking is where and when the actors move about on stage.

Character A character is a person in a play who is interpreted and performed by an actor.

Chorus In Greek drama, the chorus was a group of characters that described and commented on the action of the play, often by singing and dancing. In contemporary drama, characters can play the role of the chorus by giving information that helps to tell the story.

Cliffhanger This happens at the end of a scene when there is a feeling of 'what happens next?' There may be a precarious situation, a shocking revelation, or a dilemma to be faced.

Colloquial This refers to a style of language that is informal. It is often used to describe the way we speak rather than write. The teenagers in *DNA* often use colloquial language.

Commission In the world of theatre, a writer gets a commission when he or she is given a paid job to write a play. Dennis Kelly was commissioned to write *DNA* through the National Theatre's New Connections project.

Dialogue In drama, dialogue refers to the speaking that occurs between characters.

Director The director is the person who is in charge of the artistic aspects of a play. He or she works with actors to decide on how characters are portrayed, and also with other staff such as the play's designers and technicians.

Duologue A duologue is a part of a play with two actors speaking.

Ensemble An ensemble refers to a group of actors in a play where each character plays a roughly equal role. In *DNA*'s wood scenes, although one or other of the characters take the lead at times, the ensemble is involved in the action.

Epiphany When a person or character suddenly realizes something, or something important is revealed to them. Leah has an epiphany when she realizes that if you change one thing you can change the world.

Inciting incident An event that happens in a drama that begins the plot of a story. In the case of *DNA*, the inciting incident is the apparent death of Adam.

Monologue A monologue is a part of a play with one actor speaking.

Naturalism In theatre, naturalism is a style of drama that tries to create the illusion of reality on stage. It is a style associated with the plays of late-nineteenth-century playwrights Anton Chekhov and Heinrik Ibsen. *DNA* is not a wholly naturalistic play, but it does contain some naturalistic elements, such as the way the characters speak.

Objective A character's objective is what he or she wants to do or achieve by the end of the play. It is often their reason for behaving in a certain way. When rehearsing a play, actors will often prepare by using objectives to work out how their character speaks and behaves to get what they want.

Offstage action This refers to events that the audience does not see on stage, but have happened in the time that elapses between scenes. The planting of the DNA evidence for example is carried out offstage.

Plot The plot is the series of events that make up a story. Often, events in a plot relate though cause and effect. The word narrative can also be used for this series of events.

Production A production is a particular version of a play. Over the years since it was first performed in 2007, *DNA* has had many different productions in schools and theatres.

Props Props are objects used by actors in the play.

Revelation An unknown or surprising fact that is disclosed to others. Richard reveals to the other characters and to the audience that there is DNA evidence linking a man to Adam's disappearance.

Set The set is the environment that is made on stage in which the play is acted. This is a real space inhabited by actors.

Setting The setting is the place or places in which the imagined world of the play takes place. In *DNA*, the set must create the idea of the field, wood and street settings.

Sound effect This is a noise used as part of a performance. Sound effects can be pre-recorded and played by the technician, or made on stage by the actors themselves.

Stage direction Stage directions are lines in the play that give instructions to the actors and directors. They can refer to the setting of the scene, indicate a pause or movement, or suggest to actors how they might say a line.

Subtext This is meaning that is not stated explicitly – when a character does not say what they think or feel directly, but suggests or implies a meaning. Subtext can be read in both dialogue and actions. When Leah spits out Phil's sweet she does not explicitly reject him and the group, but it is possible to infer this meaning from the action because of the subtext it contains.

Theme In literature or drama, a theme is an idea that recurs or comes back.

Tone The tone is the mood, feel or quality of a piece of literature or drama.

CHAPTER TWO

Behind the Scenes

Dennis Kelly (playwright)

MI: One of the things I greatly admire in your dialogue is its incredible pace and energy. Can you explain how you go about creating the dialogue?

DK: I like rhythm in theatre. Because the audience is so far away compared to TV or film, the actors need to express themselves visually. You're quite a distance from the stage. Rhythm inhabits an actor's body and makes them move. Our rhythms are really the things that tell us how we feel. It's not just the words. I tend to write theatre by hand. I think that helps with rhythm. In those early plays, I wanted it to sound real. I wanted it to be rhythmic, but not for people to notice it. You want it to be slightly heightened, but also to sound natural. The best performers understand that you have to learn every single word. When actors don't learn the words properly, they can get lost on stage.

MI: Did you try to get an authenticity to the teenagers' voices?

DK: I tried not to put too much specific voice in there, because it was written for the Connections programme. I knew that there was going to be a vast range of schools doing it.

I didn't write an accent in it for example. And in the play I even specified that you could change the genders. I saw it at an all girls school and an all boys school and it worked ok. I wasn't writing for teenagers, I was writing for actors. They really like things to be hard. This is the same if you're Ian McKellen, or a fourteen year old in a school. I wrote it like any other play. It didn't matter if the play worked or if it succeeded, or really if the people watching it liked it. It was really about the people that were doing it.

MI: Was the play inspired by anything real or a real incident?

DK: Not really, there wasn't one particular event. But when we were doing it there was a story about a lad who had been chased through a housing estate by some guys with weapons and they killed him. It had gone on for a few hours and no one had done anything. The more they got away with it, the worse it got. That kind of reminded me of violence when I was at school. There's a thing that happens with violence. You do something, and you break a taboo and you don't get stopped, and then you're emboldened to take the next step. And that's what happens in the play. They're punching him, and he's laughing, and nothing stops them, and they take the next step.

MI: In many ways *DNA* seems quite timeless and placeless, but is it linked to the 2000s?

DK: Yes definitely. In our culture there is an ongoing debate about civil liberties, and whether we curtail the rights of individuals to save the many. At one moment, Phil asks if one person is more important or all of us. In an alternative universe somewhere there is another version of the play, where Phil's plan works. He takes a bunch of people who generally don't seem to be that bad, and who've make a terrible, terrible mistake, but they're kids. And there's a version of the play where he saves them. Of course that's not the version I wrote.

The play asks how much do the rights of the individual matter compared to the group. And it's a debate we're having even more now. Look at what's happening with the Extremism bill.

MI: What are your ideas on DNA linked to thematically?

DK: The DNA is linked to what kind of human beings we are. We talk about having traits in our DNA, but that's probably not really true. Traits are socially created too. But we still talk about it as if traits are in our DNA. I wanted to ask what is at the heart of our DNA. I tend to think positive things actually, in spite of what the play might suggest.

MI: Were you writing for or about young people specifically?

DK: I don't see a difference. I've even written for younger people than this. The difference between me and a five year old is that they are smaller than me. They're not stupider than me. They might know less stuff than me, but human beings are born with incredible capacities to work each other out. The people who are in this play and who are watching this play are super smart. I was writing for people rather than a different species.

MI: There are no adults in *DNA*. Was *Lord of the Flies* an influence on you?

DK: Yes definitely. There are no adults in it, because when I was this sort of age I felt the world was terrifying. Being at school was a dangerous and frightening place. There was a new kid just at school who changed my group of friends who'd all got on well. Within about six months we'd become what I thought of as a pack, and if you were close to the centre you were safe, but towards the outskirts was terrible, and being on the outside was really frightening. As a child I knew that adults had very little to do with our world. If I had a problem, if I took it to my mum she'd probably give me a slap. If you took it to a teacher you were finished. Any problems you had to deal with yourselves. When I first read *Lord of the Flies* I was probably the age of the kids in the play. I loved the clear understanding from the writer about how kids liked that worked. There's another book called *I'm the King of the Castle*, about how terrifying and serious it can be as a child. It's really serious, and you're figuring things out for yourself. Those influences were conscious influences in everything I've ever written. It was definitely deliberate that there were no adults in the play, and that they could not be rescued by adults.

MI: Can you explain why Leah and Phil spend so much time together?

DK: Phil is very simple. He just likes food because it's simple. He knows he's just got two years left and then he's out, and he can be an adult. Phil has decided he's just gonna eat, and not get involved. Phil's biggest mistake is putting the Coke can down. Once he's done that he's finished. In Leah he has found someone who just lets him be who he is. Their relationship seems dysfunctional but actually in some ways it's very functional. They both get a lot from it. She gets to project all of this stuff onto Phil. She's a talker. And she's a thinker. It's very easy to imagine that she talks too much and she gets things wrong. But she's really smart. She's very angsty. Because he does nothing she is able to project away, and he is able just to eat his food. If he hadn't put the Coke can down they could have carried on.

MI: Why did you keep the violence offstage?

DK: Violence is very difficult to get right on stage. But also I didn't want the play to become about the violence. It's more about the cooperation between them. There's an ongoing debate that humanity has about what kind of beings we are, which is in the heart of the play. You know, bonobos versus chimps. Are we inherently violent, or not? My view is that any kind of objective look at our species would have to conclude that violence, murder, genocide, war, is part of what our species does. But the other side is society, which is a beautiful thing that we have created, that stops us doing appalling things to each other. This ongoing debate goes back and forth. Having violence in the play would have coloured it too far towards saying we are violent people. We also cooperate. Although it's also true that we can cooperate to be cruel!

MI: Yes, the only violence we see on the stage is when Cathy slaps Brian.

DK: Yes. I don't see the characters as different from any I've done in any of my plays. They don't behave any better or any worse. We can have an idea about teenagers that they are scary and dangerous. I didn't want violence in because I didn't want it to be about how dangerous or awful teenagers can be. It's really about people. They're no different from you or me. We can all do violent or amazing things. It's not a case of being good or bad people. It's linked to time. One minute I can be a total idiot, the next I can be lovely.

Anthony Banks (commissioner and director)

MI: Did you know much about Dennis Kelly's writing before *DNA*?

AB: Dennis didn't start writing until he was in his late twenties. He'd had a bit of a life before he got going in theatre. I went to see an early reading of *Our Teacher Is A Troll* and I absolutely adored it. I thought his was an incredibly alive, edgy, and crunchy voice, who really understands how children characters have the capacity to portray 'good' and 'bad' and how that can be exciting for an audience. The play goes to places of pure mischievous evil with a mature humour – I thought this voice could be great for Connections.

MI: How were you involved in developing the play for Connections?

AB: The first draft really made me hold my breath – it was as if he'd written it in a fever overnight! It was electric, but it needed a few notes about the plot points in the play. I thought it was ferocious and hilarious and perfect for young people, both on and off stage. Dennis had tapped into a mainline artery of what it is to be a teenager – the temperature of it and the rhythm of it, and the way the blood can go up and down in adolescence.

MI: What is exciting about Dennis's writing?

AB: As a theatre-writer, Dennis understands two really crucial things: one, what an audience needs to keep their consciousness and imaginations whirring; two, that the theatre he creates is essentially and absolutely about words and actors. He'd thought very carefully and clearly about what would be exciting for teenage actors to perform on a stage. He came up with a story about teenage characters experiencing extreme incidents. Young people love stories which are rich in extreme incident and so do audiences; it really hooks them in.

MI: Did you face any challenges in casting the play?

AB: I drew sketches of each character and made lists of their qualities and I asked myself who they reminded me of when I was sixteen. Kids who were in my class at school all had different qualities associated with them, and I thought about this when the actors came in for their auditions. The hardest part to cast is Leah, because you have to find someone that looks like a sixteen year old who can hold an audience's attention with those technically very long and difficult speeches in very large theatres. I cast actors who were in their twenties, but who clearly had a glint of Peter Pan mischief in their eyes.

MI: Are the characters individuals or types?

AB: I think it would be a simplistic and scientific reading of the play to say that the characters are types – they've got real life-blood in them. Throughout the arc of the play's action we witness a chemistry between those characters which shows mucky push and pull. Before, after and during the scenes. They realign themselves according to circumstances. And by realigning themselves in terms of allegiances their types change. So someone who starts off as 'the bully' is not the bully by page ten or whatever, or you hear from Leah that they have changed.

MI: Did you and the actors think back to your own teenage years as part of your process?

AB: Dennis told me, 'Don't forget that these characters are my idea of what a teenager is.' What we weren't doing was a photographically naturalistic drama about sixteen year olds. I found this particularly helpful for the scenes with Leah and Phil. They are contemplative and conversational scenes, and to direct those scenes I actually thought of older couples, grandparents who sit in two chairs, eat snacks and drink tea, and one of them talks non stop and you don't know if the other one is listening or not.

MI: Do you agree with Dennis that the characters can be played by either gender?

AB: Not fully. I think at its core the genders are quite carefully placed. Leah is a kind of generous, giving, submissive girl. Phil is the strong silent type of young man probably prone to depression. Cathy is sparky, probably a bit unglued. Head Girl? Dennis wrote the play for NT Connections, which seeks to commission and develop new plays that could be performed by youth theatres, so he means it when he says the characters could be played by a boy or a girl. Like Shakespeare's plays, it has the muscle in it to be pulled in different directions in terms of gender. I'd love to see two girls or two boys do Leah and Phil. Our perception of the gender of the characters is as much about our shared references which we bring to the play as it is about the characters themselves.

MI: What were the challenges of working with an ensemble?

AB: Casting is crucial. You have to guess whether actors are going to be good in a room with other people. We were really lucky that we had eight actors who became a kind of family for each other. They were away from home on tour for six months, so it was really important that they supported each other. And they did. The best thing that happened in the first week is that we improvised for three hours without coming out of character the scene of what happened to Adam, where he is made to run across the motorway, and to set fire to himself, and to fall down the grille. We actually acted all that out. And we did it in real time. The actors had to really rigorously imagine what those kids were doing. It was a really bonding experience, because the actors understood how horrible it was. But in the acting it's a mistake to play the aftermath of the play during the play. In one performance I saw when the play was on tour the actors had really pushed the emotions, and the characters were all crying. I had to give them notes. These characters are inexperienced, unsophisticated, because they haven't got much life experience. They do not have an adult vantage point.

MI: And then the characters are just scared of getting found out aren't they?

AB: Yes. There's probably a very simple cause and effect thing that child psychologists will know about. There comes a point at puberty where you are told, 'This is the control system that the human race conforms to and operates within. If you rebel or even just step outside of that you're going to have your wrists slapped. Or you're going to be told that you're wrong. Or bad.' That is the context that the play begins in. They've all just finished puberty, and they know that what they did in the wood that day was wrong. Rather than say, 'We're bad', they want to be good. So they commit a worse crime in order to sustain their goodness. They break the rules, but make up a new set of rules themselves to right the wrong that they did.

MI: How did audiences react to the more shocking parts of the play?

AB: The cast were really careful with the way they told the story to the mainly Key Stage Four audiences that were coming to see the play. They were right to be careful, because kids in the audience were horrified by it. The two most upsetting moments were when Adam appears back from the dead, and when Phil puts the plastic bag over Brian's head. They found that quite startling. People forget that what happens in the cinema or on television has quite a different effect on the viewer to what is represented live.

MI: What is the importance of props in the play?

AB: Apart from Phil's food, only two objects are necessary: Leah's plastic lunchbox and the plastic bag used to murder Adam, which earlier in our production had contained Phil's food. They've got this bag, so that becomes the murder weapon. It's not like they have to order an automatic rifle on-line or something. The bag just happens to be there. Teenagers are spontaneous. They do things without thinking about motive and consequence. It's not like one of those plays where one of the kids has got a knife he's been secretly carrying around for weeks; its not *West Side Story*. In this one, he's just finished his sandwich, and the next minute he's a murderer!

James Alexandrou (actor, Phil, 2012)

MI: How did you approach playing Phil?

JA: I was 27 when I played Phil. That's quite a lot older than the character, but like with any other character you play it's making sure that any behavioural and physical characteristics are appropriate. You have to look at the circumstances that the character is in. You find something that makes sense to you. The thing that I do remember from that age is desperately trying to fit in, or remain part of the group, even when you're surrounded by the group.

MI: How did you make sense of Phil's character? How did you prepare for the part?

JA: Phil desperately wants a connection to other people, which he finds very difficult. It's a mistake to think that Phil is disconnected or that he is not interested. He's very isolated at the beginning of the play. And I don't know if that isolation is self-imposed. I've read from time to time that Phil is psychopathic, but that's not the whole story.

MI: Yes, in her review in *The Times* Libby Purves refers to Phil as a 'psychopathic ringleader'. Do you think this is a fair assessment?

JA: His actions can definitely be perceived as psychopathic, but then I think we all are from time to time. Psychopathy is a lack of empathy or sympathy with other people's feelings, but I think those whole bits where Leah goes on and on and on, they're not monologues. They're duologues. Or that's how I looked at them. He's listening. He's just not verbalizing his responses. Leah talks about the bonobos and chimps. It's easy to think that Phil is more chimp than bonobo, but he's actually got a little bit of bonobo. He's actually got a heart.

MI: That's really interesting, because when you read the play it's tempting to think he's just not there almost.

JA: But did you ever have that experience, at a party, and you can hear everything? You're listening, but you just can't find the words. If you're playing a character you've got to like them. You've got to find a human side. A positive version. And it's a lot more human to think that he actually wants to be there with Leah. He's actually listening really intently to what she's saying. And maybe his actions are a response to whatever's going on in her speeches. For me, he really likes Leah, throughout. I think she has a lot more sway over him than we might assume.

MI: So how do you explain what Phil actually does in the play?

JA: Phil isn't a man of words, he's a man of action. And the action he takes is one of group preservation, isn't it? It's not self-preservation. He had nothing to do with the killing of Adam. When he forces Brian to kill Adam that bit should be intensely hard to watch, and that's right. But it is for the greater good of the group. Phil is not completely amoral. The biggest compliment I had when playing Phil when was someone said they had sympathy for him. But maybe I pushed it too far. I did also come up against a bit of friction with this view of Phil.

MI: How did you cope with Phil's habit of being incredibly silent to having incredibly long speeches?

JH: Phil is a deeply thoughtful, highly intelligent person. Emotionally intelligent actually. He has to be extremely emotionally intelligent in order to be able to manipulate people in the way that he does. That was the fun of playing Phil. Those speeches can go in any direction on the night depending on where the other characters are. If Brian is in floods of tears one night, then you've won very early. Phil speaks when he needs to. Leah just speaks for the sake of it sometimes. They're complete opposites in that respect, aren't they?

MI: What choices did you make about playing the last scene?

JH: I decided not to make any decisions about the last scene, about how Phil should be. It was quite open in that way. I decided just to listen, to see how the play went that night, and just to listen to Richard. But it was a sad moment for Phil. Leah's not there now, and that's the person he's been closest to maybe in his entire life. Though Richard's filling that gap a bit.

MI: Do you think he feels guilty about what happened?

JH: I think that's maybe a speculation too far for me. Does he feel guilty? I don't know is the short answer. And that's why the play's so good. There's ambiguity there. Every decision and action he took was extremely in the moment. They come. Here's a problem. Here's a solution. The group really tortured Adam and killed him. But Phil does it as a response. You've got to look at the reality of the situation. It's a terribly intense situation. They're mucking it up, and trying to make the best of it.

MI: Was it upsetting to be in DNA night after night?

JA: Well, it's a bit naff to talk about it sometimes. But it was actually. It got very tough at times. It was a long time we were doing the play. Six months. What happens in *DNA* is horrific. By the end of the run you're formed a relationship with the character you're playing, but you can't help but consider the subject matter. It was horrible at times.

MI: Did you feel a reaction from the audience?

JA: Yeah, in the last scene, the audience was really close. Some of them had their feet on the stage. You could hear the audience gasp, and feel interest in Phil in the last scene. Which is again why it's best not to think of him as a psychopath or autistic. People who think that maybe don't like that mirror being held up to themselves. We don't like to think that under extreme circumstances we could all kill. We don't want to admit that. It's easier and safer for all of us to think that Adolf Hitler was an evil psychopath, which he probably was. But it's very hard to consider that he might have been a human being responding to situations in the worst way. That's a much darker place to take your mind.

MI: Do you have any tips for anyone putting on their own production of *DNA*?

JA: Don't take it as face value. Look at the circumstances. There's a lot more going on than meets the eye. There are a lot of plays out there that really talk down to the age group. But this one really doesn't.

Ruby Bentall (actress, Leah, 2008)

MI: How old were you when you played Leah and how did you prepare for playing a teenager?

RB: I was 19/20 when I played Leah. It was my first play, so I didn't really worry much about being a teenager because I was one. I have always looked young for my age so playing a few years younger wasn't hard.

MI: Do you think she is a typical teenager?

RB: Yeah I think she is quite a typical teenager. She's bright and clearly thinks about lots of different things when alone. She's interested in lots of things and has a curious mind. But she also has insecurities and crushes like all teenagers. Her heart is in the right place.

MI: When I first saw the play, I was struck by how intelligent Leah seemed, but also how much she was taken in by Phil.

RB: Yes she is very intelligent, but she doesn't realize. Because she talks a lot and fast, people in her life underestimate her, so she does also. Phil is the opposite. He is intelligent as well, but because he rarely speaks and doesn't jabber away he feels more intelligent. He's got more gravitas. So that wasn't difficult as an actress to play because, she doesn't realize that she is clever and thinks Phil is far superior to her.

MI: It puzzles me that Leah says she has killed Jerry and shows him to Phil? What choices did you make about this moment?

RB: My understanding of this moment is that Leah is under a huge amount of stress, feels very worried and guilty and is preoccupied with death. I think she kills him in a moment of madness and as a cry for help which is why she shows it to Phil. She needs someone to see she isn't coping and to tell her that she needs help, and also to tell her that it's all going to be fine.

MI: What was the most difficult moment to play?

RB: Leah has a huge amount of respect and love for Phil so goes along with his plans at first. As his plans get more brutal she is intelligent enough to not just be a sheep and to see that he is wrong. She however is still under his thumb enough to not run away and tell the police. It is very hard to go against the whole group. You wouldn't know if that was the right decision if everyone else was for it. I always found the bit where I had to strangle myself difficult. I always used to find it embarrassing so I don't think I ever really did it very well.

MI: What is the major turning point in the play for Leah?

RB: I think Leah's turning point is quite gradual. I think it starts after they decided to let the postman stay as a suspect.

There is a change in the next few speeches with Phil. I don't think she wants to feel like she doesn't agree with Phil, as she has spent so long telling herself that he is the most wonderful person. So in those speeches there feels more of a fakeness to her – a fake cheerfulness as though she is having to force herself to love Phil, and also a desperation because she can't bear the fact that he isn't the amazing person she thinks he is. By the time Adam has arrived back and Phil has arranged for him to die, it takes her a bit of time but she realizes that he did a terrible thing and is a bad person. Its like the spell has broken.

CHAPTER THREE

Writing About the Play

What are the Assessment Objectives?

In the examination you will have to answer a question about *DNA*. To mark your answer, the examiners will use the GCSE English Literature Assessment Objectives (AOs) specified by the Department for Education. You can look at these yourself or with your teacher (see the Bibliography of this guide for an on-line link). Here, I give some of my own advice on using the AOs and have slightly edited the wording:

AO1: Read, understand and respond to texts.

You will need to give an **informed personal response**. This means that you should have your own *opinions* about the play, but you will have to be able to back them up by showing *evidence* from it and from any wider reading and studying you have done. Giving evidence means that you need to include **details from the text and quotations.** These will help you to support your personal views and interpretations of the play. You will also need to write in a **critical style**, avoiding informal or chatty language.

AO2: Analyse a writer's language, form and structure and use relevant subject terminology.

This is where writing about the playwright, Dennis Kelly, comes in. Write about his use of techniques to create meaning or effects in *DNA*. Make sure subject terminology (eg. words such as 'tension', 'metaphor', 'irony') is used appropriately. Subject terminology needs to be relevant to your answer rather than used for no particular reason.

AO3: Show understanding of the relationships between texts and contexts in which they were written.

To cover this Assessment Objective you will need to make connections between *DNA* and what else was happening in the period it was written. There are a number of possibilities here, such as developments or concerns in society, what theatre critics or audiences thought of the play, or how other writers presented similar themes.

AO4: Use a range of vocabulary and sentence structures, with accurate spelling and punctuation.

Your own writing needs to be very clear and accurate. You will also gain credit for using a range of words and sentences well.

How can I develop and give an informed personal response?

This study guide has tried to give you some ideas about the characters, themes and the dramatic techniques that Dennis Kelly has used in *DNA*. It has suggested many points for you to discuss, and activities for you to carry out. Doing these tasks, as well as acting out extracts from the play, will help you to develop views and opinions. In discussions, you should always try to say what you think and feel. Whatever you say, your opinion will be valid, as there is never a wholly right or wholly wrong response to literature or drama. In fact, it is often perfectly fine to have a very different view from your classmates or sometimes even your teacher. Just think about Phil for example – theatre critic Libby Purves thinks he is a 'psychopath', but actor James Alexandrou who played the character, thinks he is 'emotionally intelligent' and cares deeply about the group. These views are opposites, but both are valid. Both Purves and Alexandrou are giving their view, but neither is wholly 'correct'. What do *you* think about Phil and how Kelly has presented him?

In *DNA*, there are many things you should develop a personal response about. You need to have ideas about all the *characters* and what role or function they play. What do you think of Cathy for example? How does her character serve the plot or relate to the themes of the play? You should also be ready to give your views on the play's *themes*. Kelly has written a shocking and controversial play in which a group of teenagers murder a teenage boy. What is he telling us about the way people behave? Is it that people are naturally cruel, or that they will behave irresponsibly because of peer pressure? What do *you* think *DNA* tells us about teenagers, violence and bullying?

How can I give evidence to support my personal response?

Whatever your personal responses, they must be *informed*. This means that you must give details and references from the text. If you are writing about a character, look at what they say and do. Refer to how other characters react to them or behave around them, or what they say about them. Be like a detective, and look for this evidence in the dialogue, as well as in characters' actions. Remember that you can find many clues in the stage directions.

Let's look for evidence in the second wood scene (36–8) for the following views:

(a) Cathy takes pleasure in hurting others;

(b) most of the teenagers do not deliberately want to frame an innocent man.

In the dialogue, we can find evidence that Cathy is enjoying the trouble that the group has helped to cause. When she returns from the police station with Richard, she thinks it is 'great' that it was full of reporters, and declares she is 'gonna go back' to be interviewed (36). The other characters' reactions however suggest that they are far from pleased. This is clear both in the dialogue and in Kelly's stage directions. When she reveals that they have planted evidence on a man at the sorting office, 'They all stare at Cathy', and a few lines later, 'They stare at her'. The repetition of this stage direction suggests the teenagers' surprise and shock as they take in what has happened (37–8). When Cathy tries to defend her actions, 'But isn't that . . .', she is cut off by Leah, 'No, Cathy, that is not what we wanted' (38).

To be able support your personal responses in this way, you will have to make sure that you are very *familiar with the play*. Try to make your revision active, making lists and diagrams of details, doing a flow chart to show the plot, or writing short paragraphs about each character.

Things to do

Now try finding your own evidence that supports a response to the text. Look at the last wood scene when Adam has been discovered (51–2). Highlight any evidence that shows Leah is trying but failing to take control of the situation. Explain your evidence in a pair and/or to your teacher.

How can I use quotations well?

As I have been writing this guide, I have used many quotations. You've probably noticed that many of them are very short, and sometimes they are just one word long. The quotations are often integrated into my own sentences.

Using quotations is not easy and it takes time to learn how to use them well. Try not to get frustrated if you find it tough to integrate quotations and to punctuate them correctly. Don't give up – keep trying and it should get easier.

Here are some tips to support your use of quotations:

- Remember to *introduce* a quotation. Make it clear where it comes from and who is saying it. For example, '*In Leah and Phil's first field scene, Leah asks Phil*, 'What are you thinking?' (10). You could also refer to what has been happening. For example, '*When Brian and Cathy take Adam away, Leah tries to stop them*, 'No! Stop . . .' (60). This will make your use of quotations clearer and demonstrate familiarity with the play.

- You also need to *comment on* or *analyse* your quotation. For example, 'Mark and Jan describe Adam "hanging around" and "trying to be part of" (20). *This tells us that Adam desperately wanted to be accepted by the group*.' Or, 'In the first wood scene, John Tate asks Danny, "Are you on my side?" (18). *His question reveals the tactics that John Tate uses to assert his authority*.' Notice how I am following the quotations with an interpretation or personal response.

Things to do

Now see how well you can use quotations to write about Leah. In the box above, you were asked to find evidence that Leah is trying but failing to take control of the situation when Adam has been found in the woods (51–2). Now write a short paragraph, using the quotations that you have highlighted as evidence.

In the examination, you may not be permitted to take in your play text. This will mean that you will have to remember quotations from memory. You can use different techniques to help you remember quotations, including acting lines and scenes out as if you were an actor. It helps some people to make recordings of quotations, and to listen to them through headphones. Try to be as accurate as possible with the wording of quotations, but if you find that in the examination you cannot remember the exact words, it is better to try to quote what you remember rather than not quoting at all.

How should I analyse the playwright's technique?

AO2 asks you to analyse a writer's *language, form and structure* in order to show how the writer generates meaning and effect. In other words, you will need to show *what* meanings the play communicates, as well as *how* Dennis Kelly does this in *DNA*. It will help with AO2 to think about the play from the audience's point of view. What *meanings* and *effects* are generated for them?

Think about how Kelly reveals information in the first two scenes of the play. The dialogue and action gives us *meaning*, but Kelly structures it to create *effects*. In the first scene *meaning* is generated because the audience sees two teenagers in the street discussing that someone is 'Dead' (9). The *effect* is to create tension and suspense, hooking the audience into the story. Jan's final question, 'What are we going to do?' (10) has the *effect* of making the audience want to know what will now happen. In the following scene, Leah is talking to Phil in the field. Many *meanings* are generated, as the audience learns from Leah that they have no friends, and that she is scared (11–12). Because Phil says nothing, one *effect* of the scene is that a sense of mystery is generated around his character. The audience is made to wonder whether what Leah says about Phil is true, and why he says nothing. Setting the scene in a field also creates an *effect*. The field is away from the public street, and makes the teenagers seem more distant from society.

AO2 asks you to analyse *language* too. When Mark says to Phil and Leah, 'We need to talk to you', Leah's answer is, 'Oh, shit'. Leah's abrupt expletive underlines that something very serious has happened. The audience is now even more intrigued to find out what is making the teenage characters so upset. When writing this guide I have tried to link my comments about language and dialogue to character, themes and tone. In your own examination essays on *DNA*, aim to do the same. Weave in comments about language and dialogue into your main paragraphs on character or theme, rather than separating language out into a separate paragraph.

Discuss

Use these questions to get used to thinking about effect.

1 What is the effect of the very short lines Kelly uses in Jan and Mark's scenes?

2 What effect does Mark's story about how the group bullied Adam have on the audience?

3 What kinds of effects are created by using a wood as a setting?

4 How are the audience affected when Phil gives the long series of instructions to cover up the death of Adam?

5 How is the audience affected by Leah trying to kill herself?

6 When Adam uses poetic language when telling the group what happened to him, what effect does it have on the audience?

7 What is the effect when Kelly breaks the repeated pattern of scenes he has used throughout the play in the final section?

How can I show understanding of the relationship between *DNA* and the context in which it was written?

AO3 asks you to think about the wider context in which the play was written. Although Kelly has avoided explicit references to specific times and places, you need to think about how his play shows that it comes from the 2000s. You may find useful some of the material I have included in this guide in the 'Contexts' and 'Related work' sections about life in the 2000s, adults' concerns with teenage gangs, and how other writers have portrayed teenagers.

It is important that you do not treat the context as something separate from the play. Here is an example of how to integrate a reference to context into a paragraph on Kelly's portrayal of the teenagers. 'Kelly chooses settings for *DNA* well away from school or home, teachers and parents. *Unlike other teenagers of the 2000s, whose movements were increasingly monitored through* CCTV *cameras*, members of the *DNA* gang seem to be free to behave as they like in the field and wood without being seen.'

When you are writing about the context of *DNA*, be careful with your wording. Avoid making bald statements such as, 'The character of Cathy is there because adults were worried about teenage violence in the 2000s.' Instead you may find that verbs such as 'reflect' and 'suggest' are helpful. For example, 'The violent teasing and bullying of Adam *may reflect* a social concern amongst adults in the 2000s with the behaviour of young people. Reports on gangs that operated through hierarchy and peer pressure were published in tabloid newspapers such as the *Daily Mirror*. Kelly's gang seems far from organized, and their violent or misguided behaviour is often spontaneous or unplanned.'

You can also refer to the critical response to *DNA*, as this often reflects how the play chimed with society's concerns. References to Phil as a 'psychopath' for example seem to reflect a preoccupation with crime and antisocial behaviour.

Things to do

Practise linking text and context.

- Write a paragraph about the gang's planting of DNA evidence which links to its use to fight crime and catch criminals in the 2000s.

How can I make sure I use a critical style and that my writing is accurate?

In order to do well on AO1 and AO4 you will have to pay close attention to your own writing. Written English needs to be more formal than spoken English, so be careful that you do not write your thoughts down as if you were speaking. You will have noticed that a lot of the language in *DNA* is informal, but that is because Kelly is capturing language as it is spoken by young people. You can comment on the characters' use of informal language in your examination answer, but your own language must be formal. You will lose marks for spelling and punctuation mistakes. Here are some tips for clear, formal and accurate writing.

- Spell the names of the writer and the characters correctly. For example, Dennis Kelly, not Denis Kelly. Brian, not Brien. Ask your teacher or a friend to give you a spelling test.

- Do not let your sentences get too long. It is much better to write in short, clear sentences than use sentences that never seem to end. If you find yourself relying on commas, check whether you really need a full stop.

- You will have a relatively long time to write your examination answer in English Literature. It is sensible to organize and plan your writing before you begin. Spend ten minutes brainstorming and planning your points before you start writing.

- Use paragraphs. If you have planned your work before you start writing, you will be able to start a new paragraph for each main point in your essay.

- Try to use 'drama' vocabulary where appropriate. Remember to write about characterization, stage directions, monologues, dialogue, etc. Take a look at the glossary provided in this guide to make sure you are familiar with the key terms.

- In this guide, I have used italics for the title of the play, *DNA*. In your own writing, you must show that you are referring to the title of the play either by underlining it, <u>DNA</u>, or by using inverted commas, 'DNA'. Whichever you choose, be consistent.

- When you first refer to Dennis Kelly use his full name, Dennis Kelly. If you refer to him more than once, use Kelly.

- ALWAYS leave a few minutes at the end of writing your examination answer to check your work carefully for spelling and punctuation.

- Look out for common mistakes, such as mixing up their, there and they're, or using apostrophes badly.

- Check your tenses. Do not muddle up present and past as in this sentence: 'Jan and Mark go to Phil and Leah and asked them what to do.'

Things to do

1 Make yourself a personalized spelling test, using words you find difficult or have made mistakes with in the past. You may want to include words from the glossary of this study guide. Ask a classmate or friend to test you.

2 Rewrite this rambling piece of writing on *DNA*, improving its clarity, punctuation and vocabulary. 'Dennis Kelly has written a play about a group of teenagers, who accidentally kill a boy, they meet in the woods to decide what to do and Phil, who normally just eats all the time, gives them a list of instructions, the other teenagers just listen to him.'

Answering the question

To help you answer an essay question in a focused and coherent way, you will need to construct and maintain an argument. In an essay, an argument is a set of reasons given to back up an idea or viewpoint. It is very closely linked to your personal response to the essay question.

In the examination you will be asked a question or given a task such *as 'Explore how the teenagers in* DNA *react when they think that Adam is dead.'* Your response or argument could be: 'Most of the teenagers *react* by showing dismay, anxiety and helplessness. Phil *reacts* by thinking of a plan to help the group.' Of course you may not agree with this, and have a different response to the essay question. Do notice that I have used the word *react* deliberately, as it is a key word in the essay question.

Once you have decided on your argument, you need to provide the reader of your essay with persuasive reasoning and evidence for it. Make it easier to construct your answer by planning your essay thoroughly. Start by *brainstorming points* that you want to include. These points will become your paragraphs. For example, you might want to include: 'all the teenagers go to Phil for help'; 'the leaders of the group think it is best to cover it up'; 'Brian is upset and wants to tell the truth'. When you have brainstormed your points, think about the best *order* for them. It is often helpful to follow the order they happen in the play, focusing on key moments that help to illustrate your points. You could also decide to go through your points in order of importance, writing about your most important point first.

Sometimes, you might want to make a point that qualifies your argument, or shows that the play is more complicated or ambiguous than a simple response suggests. For example, you could start a new paragraph like this

> Not all the teenagers react to the apparent death of Adam with dismay. Cathy seems to enjoy the excitement that the event has caused, and arrives in the wood '*grinning*'.

Notice how the first sentence of the paragraph links back to the essay task. Again, I have used the word *react* deliberately, to show the examiners that I am focusing on the task that they have set me. Your paragraph should then go on to give more details and quotations to show why you think that Cathy is enjoying the excitement generated by Adam's death.

A well-structured answer will have a concise introduction that tells the reader the main points of your essay. If you have spent some time planning your essay, this should make it easier to write. Do try to keep the introduction very brief – it is better to go straight into the essay than include a long rambling introduction. It is also important to keep your conclusion short. Use it to sum up your main points and highlight how you have answered the question.

Note that although you have to give a personal response to *DNA*, there is no need to use the first person. In other words, you do not need to say, 'I think that Phil responds to Adam's death by trying to help the group.' In your essay, you are presenting the end result of your thinking, so it is perfectly legitimate to say: 'Phil responds to Adam's death by trying to help the group.' If you present valid evidence to back this viewpoint up, it will be clear to the examiner that this is your informed personal response.

Writing about character

It is relatively common to be asked about character in the examination. You might have to look at how a character is presented in a particular scene, or to explore a character's journey. To write about character, you will need to provide evidence, looking for details and quotations in the dialogue at particular moments. Comment on what the character says and what other characters say about them. Also consider the character's actions very carefully, and look for clues in Kelly's stage directions.

Characters often have an objective to achieve in a particular scene. This could be for example, 'to be noticed', 'to say sorry', or 'to get money'. Objectives are useful for actors playing characters, as they will determine how the character behaves, and how they interact with other characters. For example, in their first field scene, Leah and Phil's objectives seem to be very different. Leah wants to talk to Phil, and to tell him about the things that are on her mind. She uses all kinds of different tactics to achieve this objective: she asks Phil questions, speaks at length, and tries to provoke a reaction. As Phil is silent throughout, an actor playing his part might find it harder to determine his objective. Yet the actor could decide Phil's objective is to eat and enjoy his ice-cream. This would mean that Leah and Phil's objectives conflict: Leah wants to talk, and Phil wants to eat. Objectives give the scene a sense of conflict or tension, which helps to create the drama in the scene. Identifying characters' objectives will help you to think more deeply about characters and to shape your answer in the examination.

Discuss

What are these characters' objectives in the following moments?

1 John Tate: When Richard challenges him over the use of the word 'dead' (16).

2 Mark: When he tells the group what happened to Adam (22–3).

3 Leah: When she shows Phil the contents of her Tupperware container (31–2).

4 Phil: When he explains to Cathy and Brian the 'game' with the plastic bag (58–9).

If an examination question asks you to look at a character over the course of the whole play, you will need to consider how the character develops or changes. Think about the character's starting point, their circumstances, and their objectives at the start of the play. You will need to consider the important decisions they make, or how their objectives might change. Ask yourself if the character has different objectives at different moments in the play. Structure your answer around significant moments or turning points for characters, making sure you illustrate their whole journey. Leah's objectives for example seem to be changing when she arrives in the field with a suitcase (46). Does she want to leave, or is she still trying to get Phil's attention? There is a very significant turning point for Leah in the field scene after Phil has sent Cathy and Brian off with the plastic bag. Here, she spits out the sweet given to her by Phil (61). The action shows her decision to leave Phil and the group.

Things to do

In order to track the main characters through the play, use the template below to make their profiles. This will help you to gather observations and evidence, as well as being great preparation for an examination answer. Notice how a character's role in the play – for example, to reveal information – may be different from their role or status in the group – for example, as leader or follower.

Tracking characters

	Facts, evidence and observations
Character's name:	
Role in play	
Status in group	
First appearance	
Key relationships	
Key objectives	
What other characters say about them	
How other characters treat them	
What they say to other characters	
How they treat other characters	

	Facts, evidence and observations
Key moments	1. 2. 3.
How they finish in the play	

Making comparisons

In your examination you may be given an extract and be asked to make a comparison with *DNA*. Here is an extract from Tanika Gupta's play *White Boy* (2008). The play is set outside the gates of a school, and this extract involves a group of characters: Sorted, Ricky, Zara, Shazir, Ali, Kabir and Victor. The extract begins with Sorted looking through the contents of Zara's bag.

> **Sorted** *pulls out something else from* **Zara***'s bag. It is a kitchen knife. He lays it on his lap and stares at it in awe.*
> **Sorted**   C-o-ol.
> **Ricky** *does a double take.*
> **Zara** *quickly scoops the knife up and sticks it back in her bag.*
> **Ricky**   Zara?!
> **Zara**   Protection innit.
> **Ricky**   Shouldn't be wandering 'round with a blade. . . . What you gonna do with it?
> **Kabir**   Well out of order.
> **Zara**   There's this girl in my year . . . doin' my head in . . . keeps threatening me and stuff. Thought if I carried this . . .
> **Ricky**   Get rid of it.
> **Zara**   Everyone does it.

Ricky That make it right?

Kabir He's got a point.

Shaz *opens her little dinky handbag and shows the boys a knife in her bag too.*

Sorted Cool.

Ali *looks at* **Shaz** *in horror.* **Ricky** *sucks his teeth.*

Ricky Shouldn't be messin' round with blades. You get caught or worse . . .

Sorted *suddenly scoots.*

Victor, *a black seventeen-year-old youth, carrying his school bag saunters out of the gates, texting on his phone. He stops and touches fists with* **Ricky**. **Shaz** *snaps shut her bag. Everyone else tries to talk about knives.*

Victor Yo Ricky, what's going on. Sorted on the run again?

Ricky Probably thought you were Flips.

Victor *takes the football from* **Ricky** *and plays keepie uppie with it. He virtually ignores* **Zara** *who is desperately trying to gain his attention by walking seductively up and down.*

This extract makes a good comparison with the first wood scene of *DNA*, where John Tate is trying to ban the word dead, and threatens to hurt Richard if he uses it (15–16). You might be asked, for example, about the different situations the groups are in; to explore the relationships and power dynamics of the scenes; or about how the language and actions of the extracts create effects.

If you have to do a comparative task in your examination, careful planning, organization and structuring of your answer will be necessary. Here is a list of pointers to help you.

- Make sure you read the examination question and any bullet points you are given extremely carefully.

- Keeping the question and bullet points in mind, highlight the extracts with a pen or pencil to find the right evidence in the dialogue and the stage directions.

- Sometimes, it is helpful to use the bullet points as a topic for each paragraph, as this will help you cover all aspects of the question you have been asked.

- Do not start writing your answer until you have made a plan to organize your points.

- Look for both similarities and differences. It is often helpful to write about a simple similarity, but then to tease out the differences. For example, 'Both these passages present a group of teenagers unaccompanied by adults. Whereas the teenagers in *White Boy* are outside the school gates, the group from *DNA* meet much further away from adult supervision.'

- Remember to integrate comments on language or dramatic technique into your main paragraphs rather than cover them in a separate paragraph.

- However you organize the answer, always refer back to the question, and make sure you have answered all parts of it.

Things to do

Use the first *DNA* wood scene (15–16) and the above passage to practice a comparison question:

'How do Tanika Gupta and Dennis Kelly present the behaviour and the relationships between teenagers?'

In your essay, consider:

- the situations the teenagers are in and what they do;

- who has the power or status within the group;

- the way the teenagers speak to each other.

BIBLIOGRAPHY

About Us, http://connections.nationaltheatre.org.uk/about-us#.VYahK6YXq1k [accessed 21 June 2015].

AQA. 'New GCSE English Literature Set Texts: *DNA*'. *English GCSE News*, September 2009, 7, http://www.school-portal.co.uk/groupdownloadfile.asp?resourceid=4675415 [accessed 1 August 2015].

Arts Council England. Artistic Assessment Form, 2 May 2012.

Assessments and Qualifications Alliance. 'The Power of DNA'. *English Newsletter*, May 2012, 16, http://filestore.aqa.org.uk/subjects/AQA-GCSE-ENG-NEWS-12.PDF [accessed 18 June 2015].

Banks, Anthony. Interview with Maggie Inchley. National Theatre, 16 June 2008.

Benedict, David. 'Review: Review of *Baby Girl/DNA/The Miracle*', *Variety*, 3 March 2008, http://variety.com/2008/legit/reviews/baby-girl-dna-the-miracle-1200536141/ [accessed 24 July 2015].

Bennett, Claire-Louise. 'DNA (Deoxyribonucleic acid) by Dennis Kelly'. irish**theatre**magazine, 15 July 2009, http://www.irishtheatremagazine.ie/Reviews/Current/DNA-%28Deoxyribonucleic-acid%29 [accessed 25 July 2015].

Billington, Michael. 'Review of *Baby Girl/DNA/The Miracle*'. *The Guardian*, 10 April 2008.

Billington, Michael. 'Review of *Burn/Chatroom/Citizenship*'. *The Guardian*, 16 March 2006.

Bowie-Sell, Daisy. 'Dennis Kelly: Rioters thought there were no rules – but my characters know right from wrong', 1 February 2012, 'http://www.telegraph.co.uk/culture/theatre/theatre-features/9052744/Dennis-Kelly-Rioters-thought-there-were-no-rules-but-my-characters-know-right-from-wrong.html [accessed 7 June 2015].

Butler, Leo. *Redundant*. London: Methuen, 2001.

Department for Education, *English Literature: GCSE Subject Content and Assessment Objectives*, DfE 2013, https://www.gov.

uk/government/uploads/system/uploads/attachment_data/
file/254498/GCSE_English_literature.pdf [accessed 13 October
2015].

Gang Culture. University of Leicester, http://www.le.ac.uk/ebulletin-
archive/ebulletin/features/2000-2009/2006/08/nparticle.2006-08-
03.html [accessed 27 July 2015].

Gardner, Lyn. 'DNA – Review'. *The Guardian*, 14 February 2012.

Gordon, Rachel A., et al. 'Antisocial Behaviour and Youth gang
Membership: Selection and Socialization'. *Criminology* 42, no. 1
(2004): 55–87.

Halliburton, Rachel. 'Review of *Burn, Chatroom, Citizenship*'. *Time
Out*, 22 March 2006.

Hanna, Laurie. 'Teenage Gangs of Britain'. *Mirror Online*, 24 April
2007, http://www.mirror.co.uk/news/uk-news/teen-gangs-of-
britain-469308 [accessed 24 August 2015].

Kelly, Dennis. *DNA: School Edition*. Oberon: London, 2008.

Kelly, Dennis. *Plays Two*. London: Oberon, 2013.

Lewis, Louise. *'DNA'*, British Theatre Guide, 8 February 2012,
http://www.britishtheatreguide.info/reviews/dna-rose-theatre-
ki-7193 [accessed 27 July 2015].

Marmion, Patrick. 'Review of *Burn, Chatroom, Citizenship*'. *Daily
Mail*, 17 March 2006.

McKee, Robert. *Story*. London: Methuen, 1999.

Morley, Sheridan. 'Review of *Burn, Chatroom, Citizenship*'. *Daily
Express*, 16 March 2006.

Purves, Libby. 'Putting the Chill in Childish'. *The Times*, 6 March
2012, http://www.thetimes.co.uk/tto/arts/stage/theatre/
article3340759.ece [accessed 25 July 2015].

Shell Connections 2005: New Plays for Young People. London:
Faber and Faber, 2005.

Smith, A. S. H. *'DNA*, Rose Theatre, Kingston', the *arts*desk.com,
7 February 2012, http://www.theartsdesk.com/theatre/dna-rose-
theatre-kingston [accessed 24 July 2015].

Spencer, Charles. 'Review of *Burn/Chatroom/Citizenship*'. *Daily
Telegraph*, 17 March 2006.

INDEX